YORKSHIRE 1939–1945
The Secret War

YORKSHIRE
1939–1945
The Secret War

Ron Freethy

COUNTRYSIDE BOOKS
NEWBURY BERKSHIRE

First published 2010
© Ron Freethy 2010

COUNTRYSIDE BOOKS
3 Catherine Road
Newbury, Berkshire

To view our complete range of books,
please visit us at
www.countrysidebooks.co.uk

ISBN 978 1 84674 218 7

Designed by Peter Davies, Nautilus Design
Produced through MRM Associates Ltd., Reading
Typeset by Jean Cussons Typesetting, Diss, Norfolk
Printed by Cambridge University Press

Contents

AREA MAP

Introduction and Acknowledgements

Yorkshire is our largest county and during the 1939–45 war, its industrial might played a vital role in producing essential materials for the war effort. Men, women and also children felt the impact of the war, although thankfully the young are always happier, more optimistic and more able to cope providing they have parental support. Those who were evacuated, however, must have experienced unpleasant upheavals. Adults had to face the threat of actual invasion and the invasion of their privacy whilst at the same time having to work harder than ever before. What the war did, however, was to increase employment and this came as a relief to the industrial regions recovering from the depression of the 1930s.

This book is not intended to be an academic summary of events but a record of what it was like for those who lived in Yorkshire during these desperate times. As such I have relied on personal memories and I am grateful to the local media who advertised my pleas for contributions from those who were 'in the thick of it'.

I must also thank local libraries and museums, and my special thanks go to the archive staff of the York Railway Museum, Sheffield Library and Leeds Library. With regard to Leeds Library, I am particularly grateful for the help I was given by Michel le Fevre in the Reference Section.

For information in Chapter 6 – War at Sea, I must thank Lionel Marr whose family owned trawlers in Hull.

I also became an avid reader of the works of Alec Gill and those who want a more in-depth account of Hull at war should consult Alec's website or 'google' him; his books on the subject are a delight.

Finally, I must thank my wife for her word processing skills, her patience and her ability to work as my taxi driver. Of course, any author needs the help, encouragement and skills of his or her publisher and in this respect the Countryside Books team have served me well.

The last word must go to my readers and I hope that if they have their own memories to share, they will write to me, c/o Countryside Books, so that these can be added to an expanding archive of material on 'Yorkshire at War'.

Ron Freethy

Chapter 1

Repel All Boarders

Contrary to much that has been written, Britain was better prepared for war than most recent commentators and writers have suggested. Invasion preparations were in hand all over Britain prior to the outbreak of hostilities and Yorkshire's secret plans were no exception. Indeed, the people of Yorkshire and the East Coast were more aware of the threat than most.

At Scarborough, for example, the harbour is often strewn with fishing nets, crab pots and lobster pots, with the whole area dominated by the lighthouse. The original 19th-century structure was destroyed on 16th December 1914 by gunfire from two German warships and brought a sharp reminder that the Royal Navy was not always able to provide coastal protection. In the context of this book we should remember that the replacement lighthouse had controlled the harbour traffic for less than 20 years when the next war loomed.

Furthermore, in 1915, soldiers from the Manchester Regiment were killed by a Zeppelin attack. This was not in Manchester but on the Lincolnshire coast when the troops were guarding an

important radio station, but events like this were not forgotten by the folks of the East Coast and true Yorkshire grit was much to the fore as plans were formulated to repel boarders! Instructions were issued in great secret and these were passed on only to those who 'needed to know'. Invasion conferences were held behind closed doors with those present including police chiefs, civilian town hall officers, especially town clerks, and of course the mayors. There was also a vital military presence and a prominent member of what was in those days a voluntary fire service.

Each of these bodies was given a confidential 26-page document issued by the Home Secretary's Office and entitled *Consolidated Instructions to Invasion Committees of England and Wales* (it must be assumed from this that Scotland had its own secret system). The broad thrust of the anti-invasion plan was as follows:

1. The names, addresses and telephone numbers of the committees and other local people who needed to know were noted and kept in a secure place. There were designated War Rooms set aside which could become functional very quickly.

2. There was a successful plan to involve local people with a knowledge of locks – and who were able to keep their mouths even more firmly shut! One such man was remembered by Joyce Parrington: 'My father, who was a builder by trade, had two hobbies. These were inventing things and breeding Siamese cats. It was one of these cats which saved dad's life and why I can tell you about his contribution to Yorkshire's 'Secret War'. Before the war he specialised in designing strongrooms, especially for banks but also for storing sensitive documents. He was obviously in great demand as the war clouds gathered. I know that he spent a lot of time around Liverpool when the control room for the Navy was being planned in preparation for the war in the Atlantic. We lived close to the docks of Hull and although we were away he was at home one night when he missed his favourite cat. Despite the fact that the siren had sounded, he left the safe place in the basement and went into the long garden. A bomb hit the house and dad was blown off

his feet. As he was gathering his senses he heard a purring as his cat curled up on his chest – he said that it was not just cats which had nine lives! He lived until he was 94 and he still kept designs he had drawn up for the pillboxes which one of his companies erected up and down the Yorkshire coast. He certainly passed on his enthusiasm to my brother and me. We both became architects and we both love our cats!'

John Parrington, with his favourite cat. It was John who felt he had nine lives, escaping injury when a bomb hit his house.

3. Statistics and facts relating to the local population, houses, buildings and resources of the area were listed so that use could be made of this important information by the relevant Invasion Committee. Some of these details are in local archives but they were so secret that many have been 'lost'. There are, for example, no details relating to Leeds despite diligent searches by myself and the staff of Leeds Reference Library, with Michel Le Fevre being very supportive of the project.

4. There were very detailed arrangements for liaising with the civil and military authorities, with the proviso that should there be a German landing the military would be very firmly in command, but the public were to be kept informed and told exactly what to do.

5. Of the utmost importance, was a published chain of command to be put into operation immediately an invasion force looked

to be on its way. A secret document labelled *Invasion Instructions* was to be kept handy but placed under lock and key in the designated War Room.

6. A list of locally-approved code words was to be issued, including dialect words and the names of sports events and individuals with regard to football and especially to the Rugby League hotbeds around Hull and West Yorkshire. Cricket heroes were also to be included. There were also lists of local people bearing Germanic names, which resulted in a careful watch being kept on many innocent people, as Ernest Schultz recalls with some humour though it must have annoyed him at the time.

He wrote to me in 2009: 'I'll bet you did not expect to hear from a Nazi whilst writing about the Secret War in Yorkshire! Let me explain. I was born and bred in Bradford and spoke with a broad Yorkshire accent, but my family came from Germany in the 1870s when many German merchants settled in Bradford in connection with the wool trade. Germany was a major importer of Yorkshire textiles and we had our own warehouses in Bradford. The area where we lived is still called 'Little Germany' and we had our own church. Within a couple of generations we were more English than German.

'Obviously German names caused suspicion in the First World War and many changed their names and some fought on the British side and died in the trenches. My family kept our name and we still do

Ernest Schultz, who describes himself as a proud 'Tyke Kraut'.

13

even though I am nearly 90 and my sons are still British in persuasion but genetically have German blood. I was born in 1927 and just ready to start university when Hitler started his tricks. I wanted to join the RAF but when my name appeared I was taken to a separate room and given a very firm grilling. My father and my younger brothers and sisters were almost sent to the Isle of Man and classed as aliens but common sense prevailed and my father was allowed to continue working as a textile chemist. The younger children were bullied a little at school and it took time for the dust to settle. We all noticed that our identity papers were more carefully scrutinised than those of fellow travellers and my father was allowed to do fire watching but was not allowed to join the ARP (Air Raid Precautions). I did eventually join the British Army and fought in Italy, becoming a sergeant and affectionately known to my troop as 'Kraut'. I hope that you publish this letter in full and allow me to sign myself as a Faithful British Kraut.'

I can do no less than quote this Tyke Kraut's letter in full and it shows how wars can divide nations and yet eventually the wounds of conflict are healed.

7. A chain of command including the Home Guard and all of the specially trained units to be described in Chapter 3 were to be brought into action, and those recruited in secret and who evolved the techniques of sabotage into a fine art – or should it be a science? – were to be activated.

At this time the police force would certainly have become over-stretched and here the ARP wardens had a crucial part to play. All wardens were given their orders in secrecy and were equipped with Air Raid Precautions Training Manual No. 3, for which they were obliged to pay the princely sum of one penny! This is not so silly as it first appears: in black print there was a note to say that 'Copies will only be sold only on written application to H.M. Stationery Office, York House, Kingsway WC2 by a Principle of a Public Utility Company or Industrial or Commercial Concern.' This document was marked 'Confidential' rather than 'Secret' but it was obvious that the Home Office wanted to tell people how to react to the presence of an invasion force, and the less the enemy knew of these instructions the better.

In Yorkshire, the most vulnerable area was along the coastal strip between Whitby and Hull but it was considered possible that there would be paratroop units landing in inland areas too. It was unlikely that the whole invasion force would land until a long period of bombing and dive-bomb attacks had taken place, a tactic the Germans had employed with success against the almost defenceless Poles.

This accounts for the distribution of pillboxes, which were not built in any haphazard fashion but were part of a well-planned network guarding all strategic roads. Obviously there were many situated around beaches, ports and docks but the defensive network also extended into country areas. There is one surviving box on the road between Hebden Bridge and Nelson which was one of many which linked to the Lancashire system. The defence of Britain quite rightly paid no attention to artificial county boundaries.

What is certain is that the defensive arm of Northern Britain was both long and well organised from 1937 onwards. In my time at BBC Television I worked with and became friends with Eric Halsall, who made his name as a presenter of *One Man and His Dog*. Eric lived in the village of Cliviger, between Burnley and Todmorden on the Yorkshire border. We had many conversations, mainly about sheepdogs but also about the orders he was given in the event of a German invasion. Eric

Eric Halsall – an 'up hill and down mines' man.

15

grinned as he told me, 'I suppose I've always been an "up hill and down mines man". I earned my living as a coal-mining engineer in the Yorkshire pits and like many miners I craved a breath of fresh air in my spare time. This is when my love of sheepdogs developed.'

I knew that he loved sheepdogs because every time I enjoyed a cup of wonderful tea made by Eric's wife, his dog sat on my lap and looked hard at Eric as if to say, 'When are we going to work some sheep?'

Eric continued: 'When it looked as if invasion was imminent I was called to a meeting with a number of other mining engineers. The secret chap we met was keen on two things. Firstly he wanted to keep the mines open as long as possible but if the Germans came then the mines were to be sabotaged. We all had to sign the Official Secrets Act and make two lists. The first list was of old mines which could be used to hide specially trained troops of what later became the Home Guard. They were interested in the very old drift mines which did not require shafts operated by machinery, which we were to blow up anyway. The second list was of young, fit miners who understood explosives but who were also not known to have any violent left-wing sympathies.'

These drift mines, often with closed-in entrances which only had to be camouflaged, were indeed manned by brave volunteers. They were divided into groups of between six and eight men and the shafts were equipped with rations for five or six days. When ordered, the men were to go underground and be given the best radio equipment then available. They were really suicide squads with orders to attack German targets 'at whatever risk'. Eric Halsall's point was that miners with left-wing sympathies were not to be contacted, but this changed when the Germans attacked Russia. The units were not finally disbanded until late in 1944.

The secret investigations of suitable men like Eric Halsall were surprisingly thorough, as Eric himself told me: 'At the end of that first meeting I was taken to meet another chap who looked like a clone of the other. At first all he wanted to talk about was sheep and then he asked me how well I knew the area where I worked my dogs, judged the trials and how well I knew the shepherds. He finally made his point. I was to tour areas, meet shepherds and also if possible quarrymen and to make sketch maps and select areas where small groups of troops could hide away in the event of invasion. I was to pay special attention to railway lines, road junctions and especially bridges. On no account was I to tell anybody anything.'

Two sides to every story

When we think of the secret war in Yorkshire we should not forget that there are two sides to each and every conflict. The Germans had a network of spies under the guise of tourists or 'courtesy visitors' from the early 1930s onwards. Many may well have remained after war was finally declared. It was right that in the 1940s the 'loyal tykes' should trust nobody and say nowt. The Luftwaffe well knew where the industrial areas were, what was being produced and how they could be disrupted by bombing. Sheffield steel was high on their priority list and all aircrew were provided with aerial maps. This accounts for two aspects of the secret war – ARP wardens were told to be ruthless and prosecute people who refused to 'put that light out', and the so-called Operation Starfish involved building mock industrial complexes out of wood and lighting these up when bombers were approaching to create a diversion.

Sheffield was then, and still is to some extent, a city of steel – or more accurately, a city of iron and steel. Here there were gargantuan foundries and steel rolling mills which produced among many other things, anchors, cables, propeller shafts, boilers, armour plate, big guns, turbines, railway lines and pipework. The Germans were probably not interested in the silver plate or cutlery industry but they well knew that if they devastated Sheffield, Britain's war effort would be severely disrupted.

In this context it is of interest to quote an article printed in the *Daily Herald* in May 1937. Its headline was 'Nazis must be Spycalists', and it described cycling tours of Britain by the Hitler Youth. They had apparently been told: 'Impress on your memory the roads and paths, villages and towns, outstanding church towers and other landmarks. Make a note of the names of places. Perhaps you may be able to utilise these sometime for the benefit of the Fatherland.'

These cyclists for some reason were allowed to tour all the factories around Sheffield. If this was not spying I would like to know what it was!

'Steeling' a march on the Germans

From the 1840s onwards and probably before then, the scientists intent upon improving the quality of steel were dominated in turn by Germans and the men from Sheffield. They guarded their secrets jealously and this became ever more closely focused in the two world wars.

The men from Sheffield fought their own 'Secret War' and the Luftwaffe targeted the steel city and no doubt had spies at work in locating the most important production sites. In 1940, for example, the Vickers Armstrong-owned furnace was the only one which could make the stress-resistant crankshafts for the Rolls-Royce Merlin engines and the hammer which forged them was under armed guard day and night, while the room that housed it was strengthened to resist all bombs save a direct hit. This factory also made disks for the developing jet engines and the drop forgings for the aircraft produced by the Blackburn Company, which is fully described in a later chapter.

The Germans could not have failed to notice that hardly a military or a civil aircraft existed which did not contain at least one part which could only have been made in Sheffield. Lord Beaverbrook's advice to Winston Churchill was not to put all the industrial eggs in one basket and he devised a system of 'shadow factories'. This involved having several factories producing the same thing so that one bomb attack would not destroy the whole production line. One notable exception in Sheffield's case was the 'Merlin crankshaft hammer' and hence the cloak of secrecy which surrounded it.

Mike Spick, who is the Education and Outreach Officer at Sheffield Library, pointed me in the right direction and I was able to study the blitz of the steel city from a knowledge of the targets which the Luftwaffe were aiming at. There is an archive of more than 400 images of the 1940's blitz entitled 'Citizens Coping', which, as in all Britain's cities, they most certainly were.

Apart from aircraft, Sheffield has often been regarded as the arsenal of England and ships' rudder frames, propellers and shafts, turbine drums and boilers were all made in Sheffield and were often forged in one huge piece which then had to be transported by rail and road in great secrecy and often at night with lights kept as dim as possible. Driving these huge items took both skill and nerve and both men and women played their part. Armour plating and huge guns were also produced and had to be transported to construction sites all over the country.

The firm of Husbane and Company produced high quality polished steel which was later used for the reflector for the ground-breaking telescope at Jodrell Bank in Cheshire. During the war the factory was involved in the evolution of VHF radio and the ever-improving radar installations.

Both sides in the war were well aware of the value of high quality steel and any invasion plan would have involved massive airborne landings in order to secure strategic targets. This is why two plans were formulated. Firstly attempts were to be made to repel the enemy, hence the network of pillboxes. If this failed, then sabotage teams were organised and briefings prepared in minute detail.

This is often forgotten as attention has been concentrated upon coastal defences, which were obviously needed to combat the brunt of the main invasion force. Some of these installations can still be seen to this day.

A number of observation posts were set up at strategic points; one of the most prominent being at Flamborough Head, one of my favourite strolls with magnificent views far out to sea. This was obviously why it was selected way back in late 1937. Situated between Bridlington and Filey bays, Flamborough Head juts out into the sea and was therefore a perfect observation point in the event of an invasion. The name Flamborough means 'Flein's Burg', which comes from the Old Norse personal name of Flein. From the

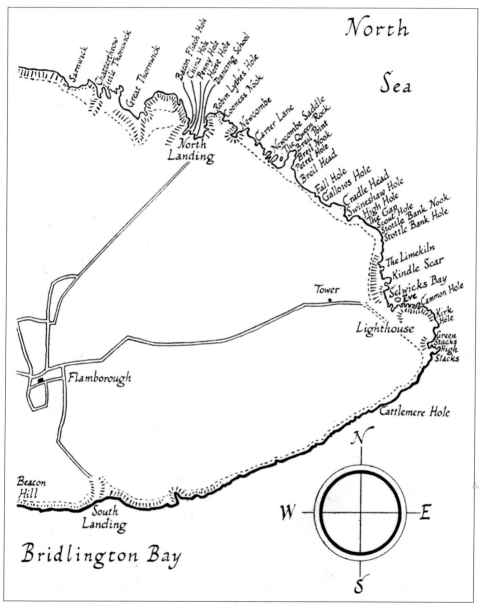

Map showing the observation points at Flamborough Head.

time when we were invaded by the Vikings, sightings from this headland have been an early warning of a threat to come.

There are bays here which had to be protected from invasion by the Germans, notably South Landing, Selwick Bay, North Landing and Great and Little Thornwick. Caves were strengthened to produce 'natural pillboxes', while the lighthouse built by John Matson for Trinity House in London in 1806, with its 87 ft high circular tower and standing 214 ft above sea level, was the perfect place to watch for raiders not just from the sea but from the air. No wonder its defences were kept secret.

The same cloak of secrecy covered the pre-war activities around Hornsea Mere, which is the largest freshwater lake in Yorkshire, formed during the Ice Ages and gouged out by glaciers, and situated only ¾ mile from the North Sea. It covers 467 acres (191 hectares), is 2½ miles long, ¾ mile wide at its broadest point and is only 12 ft deep and 12 ft above sea level. It has sluice gates and a piped outlet to the sea. It has long served as a fishery, a nature reserve and a base for a sailing club.

In the First World War it was an important seaplane base which must have been well known to the Germans. Hornsea would have been a vital part of the Nazi invasion plan. The five-mile circular path around the mere was suddenly out of bounds and the mere was surrounded by barbed wire, a complex of obstructions and an impressive military presence. In the cold winter of 1940 the water froze solid and the off-duty troops enjoyed learning to skate using bits of iron strapped to their boots.

The area of the Humber estuary was also of vital importance and its defences were strengthened. Preparations were made early, as Nigel Woods told me:

'When we arranged to meet I thought you wanted to talk about me and the war in Yorkshire. I could not understand how I could contribute because I was a bomber navigator flying out of Lincolnshire. Unlike most bomber men I never got a scratch but I lost many good mates. It is my family connection which you need to know about. We were a mixed lot – all equally intelligent I think, but whilst I eventually taught maths all over Yorkshire my cousins have wrongly been described as manual workers. This was an insult as my cousin Gerald Woods was a skilled carpenter and his brother was an electrician.

'Early in 1940 I was on leave and went with Gerald to Spurn Head, a haunt of ours when we were kids fishing and catching rabbits. He told me that he had a pass but I would be okay if I wore my uniform. It turned out that detailed plans had been made as the long beach at Spurn Head down to the lighthouse was expected to be a German point of landing. After a careful examination of my 1250 Form, which is the RAF identity card, I was let past the checkpoint. A new road was being built, there were pillboxes everywhere and huge concrete blocks placed so that they acted to deter the movement of tanks. A team of Royal Engineers were fiddling about around the new road and would obviously have blown it up if the Germans had gained a bridgehead. I was introduced to Gerald's boss who was an army major and there was a sophisticated and obviously very secret observation system going on.'

Since the 1970s, as part of my work as a naturalist, I have visited Spurn Point because the area is now a reserve run by the Yorkshire Wildlife Trust. Visitors stay in huts which were built for the garrison in 1940 and there are bird hides in strategic places. In 1940 eyes were skinned for an invasion fleet whilst nowadays binoculars search the sea on the look-out for rare birds. A walk around the area reveals lots of concrete tank blocks and little hideaways which these days keep the winds at bay rather than deflecting bullets!

All of these one-time secret installations can now be described but many events have been lost forever. A few secret plans involving individuals have survived the pressures of time. I spoke to Ailsa Buxton, now living on her barge near Stratford-on-Avon. She told me: 'I've lived on or around canal barges all of my life. My family worked their own barge along the Leeds to Liverpool Canal from at least the 1850s. Our whole life was spent on board except when we kids were forced to go to school. I still have family photographs showing the barges at work and our living accommodation which

Ailsa Buxton, whose grandfather played a part in the 'secret' war.

had a warm stove and was very comfy. But this is not what you want to know about.

'During the war my grandfather, who was too old to work the barges from our base in Bingley, was suddenly given an old barge tucked away in a disused bit of canal on the Rochdale Canal near to Sowerby Bridge, close to Halifax. His barge was made very comfy and had a small paraffin heater and a big radio. Later he told us that all he had to do if invasion came was to sit as if he was fishing and then if he saw owt he were to report his findings to a central control somewhere in Leeds. My grandad's memories were not just of a secret war but also a silent war because thankfully he never had to use the radio as the Germans never came. He did, however, see or rather hear bombers on their way

The Leeds to Liverpool Canal where the Buxton family plied their trade

to Leeds and in the 1940s Blitz he was joined for a while by a chap from the Royal Observer Corps who reported on aircraft movement. One thing grandad was good at was keeping his mouth shut and all he would do if we asked him what was in his barge was to light another fag!'

Obviously the anti-invasion plans had to be kept secret but the way that Yorkshire organised its civil defence meant that all activities needed to be planned with a high degree of secrecy and this is the subject of the next chapter.

Chapter 2

The Home Front and Civil Defence

When we think these days of the Home Front in the Second World War, we think of the comedy television programme *Dad's Army* which has become part of British folklore. There was much more to the Home Front than just the Home Guard, however, and there was plenty of activity by the police force, the ARP wardens and the then fragmentary Voluntary Fire Service.

These organisations kept thousands of Yorkshire folk busy during the war, with most holding down a 'day job' as well. Most attention will always be focused upon the Home Guard though, for it was a surprisingly well organised army in every sense of the word.

On 13th May 1940, just three days after he became Prime Minister, Winston Churchill delivered his now famous speech which included the phrase '*I have nothing to offer but blood, toil, tears and sweat*'. Churchill was not just good with words, he was very much a man of action. He had been involved in the Boer War in South Africa and was well aware of how effective the Afrikaaners had been in developing guerrilla groups which attacked suddenly and then regrouped elsewhere or vanished into the bush.

Anthony Eden was appointed the Secretary of State for War and asked for volunteers to join what was initially called the Local Defence Volunteers, which almost immediately became known as 'Look, Duck and Vanish'. In around a fortnight, more than 250,000 men had volunteered and local police stations and other outlets ran out of forms. Churchill himself took exception to the Look, Duck and Vanish nickname and renamed the force the Home Guard.

It would have seemed certain at that time that the units would soon see action. France surrendered on 22nd June 1940 and the Dunkirk miracle which saved so many troops still looked like the one bright spot as the German troops advanced. Churchill's battle cry, that the British would fight on the beaches and then in the hills, was taken up. Old weapons in museums and private collections were oiled and got ready for action. One farmer in Wensleydale produced no fewer than five blunderbusses and melted down lead pipes and water troughings to make very lethal-looking bullets. Wooden replicas of guns were made and even deadly-looking weapons and battle-axes from the Civil War of the 1640s were sharpened and polished. All the Home Guard men were waiting in anticipation to hear the password 'Cromwell', which meant 'prepare for action'. In the end, the RAF won the Battle of Britain – 'nobbut just' – and though the Nazi invasion was put on the back burner, the Home Guard were ordered to remain vigilant.

When I first started presenting programmes for BBC radio and television I was told always to write down details of the people I interviewed and to keep transcripts of everything that was transmitted. This avoided repetition of the same facts. I was also told that when working in television it paid to collect any relevant photographs which could be used as stills. I have interviewed many

John Warburton (right) and Albert Gillings, reunited after the war in 1946.

people along the theme 'What did you do in the war, daddy – or in some cases, mummy?' – and in the context of the present book I looked up an interview I had with John Warburton concerned with motorcycle TT racing on the Isle of Man and his other related sport of scrambling, which involved preparing motorbikes to race up and over the hills and into muddy depressions. This proved invaluable to John during the war.

John recalled: 'I earned my living from garages I had in the 1930s at Blackpool, Leeds and outside Filey. In those days we did not have supplies of spares for cars but we could either repair a broken part or even make a new one in our own workshop. I had a very clever young man working for me called Albert Gillings, who came from Great Yarmouth. He literally could mek owt to get a vehicle going. When I went racing on the Isle of Man, it was Albert who kept the machine running and running fast. Then came the war and both Albert and me volunteered.

'Albert went into the army as a driver mechanic but they told me I was too old. I had told them that I was a TT rider and I was taken into an office and interviewed by a posh chap with lots of pips on his shoulder. He told me that if an invasion came, communications might be cut and having special Home Guard chaps on motorbikes would be useful. I was sworn to secrecy and contacted every motorcycle owner I knew. Some machines were antiquated but still useful for high speed scrambling and I soon had a big team all over the east coast of Yorkshire. There were Nortons, BSAs, AJSs and lots of other makes famous in their day all tuned up and ready to meet the German threat. We held competitive races between one pillbox and the next which would obviously have been vital if the enemy had landed. As the invasion threat eased, I was employed to repair and service antiquated tractors, including some First World War vintage Fordsons. In the Blitz I remember working to restore an ancient Saunderson fire engine which was made in Bedford before the first war. One thing about them days – they built machines to last and they were easy to repair.'

There are also valuable memories of special units within the Home Guard where the men had unique skills honed in their

Even in agriculture, it was a case of 'Adapt' and 'Make Do and Mend'. In 1940 this Austin Heavy saloon of 1926 was modified to become a tractor.

'normal' employment. Derek Bowker recalled: 'In 1938 there were secret meetings with men who knew the workings of the old lead mines and smelt mills, especially around Swaledale. Many of the old workings had long underground passages and flues. There was one at Gunnerside Gill in Swaledale and another on Grassington Moor. Groups of Home Guard lads who were fit as butchers' dogs and who understood guns and explosives were divided into squads of between six and eight and taught to use radios.

'They went into the old workings and sealed off areas in which they stored rations. If the Germans gained a foothold they were to follow Churchill's advice and fight in the hills. They were to be given targets such as railway lines and bridges but they had other secret orders which told them to go where they liked and to cause

*The engineers of the Hodder and Stocks reservoir project. Edward Green is
fourth on the right on the top row.*

the maximum disruption. I know there were also some lads who
knew the railway and canal systems like the palms of their hands
and the railway lads had their own targets.'

Once the threat of invasion receded the Home Guard still had
vital work to do. They were ordered to guard important
installations and man coastal defences, thus releasing regular troops

for service overseas. Mary Postlethwaite, now living in Leeds, told me: 'I have memories of my late father-in-law, Edward Green, who worked as an engineer on the Stocks Reservoir project, which is between Skipton and Clitheroe. This reservoir was opened in July 1932 to provide water for the west coast of Lancashire.'

Mary, an ex-schoolmistress who taught Latin, suddenly adopted a Yorkshire accent as she related Edward Green's story in his own words: 'I remember it as if it were yesterday. Mr Saunders and a few more bosses came into our room and closed the door. They had called us back to Stocks in July 1939 and in the group was a chap in a suit. He looked like a solicitor, including a bowler hat. "Nah then," he said, "you lads spent years building a dam and pipelines. I'm here to tell you that you will not be called up. The first thing the bloody Germans will do is to blow up the dams and you lot are going to be trained to stop 'em. If they do invade, it will be your job to blow up everything so that the Germans can't use it." '

Mr E. Saunders, resident engineer of the Hodder Aqueduct project.

From the outset all the Home Guard units had one factor to bear in mind which did not affect regular troops. Hitler himself decreed that Home Guard recruits were not troops but civilians in revolt and as such would not be given the protection of the Geneva Convention. Those captured would either be shot on the spot or transported to concentration camps in Europe. The result was not quite what Adolf had anticipated – recruitment to the Home Guard almost doubled overnight. One Yorkshire mineworker told me, 'The buggers would have to catch us first. To quote the first war – we know a better 'ole and we'll go to it!'

In the first instance, the Home Guard was short of both uniforms and weapons. With the Yorkshire woollen mills working at full capacity in some areas, this was soon addressed and the units looked very efficient although initially short of armament. Few people realise even to this day that the American FBI had a problem which they felt the British Home Guard could solve. They had a huge arsenal of weapons and ammunition which they had confiscated from the gangsters of the 1930s, so well known to us from the old Hollywood films. Tommy guns, automatics and other lethal weapons were shipped across the Atlantic in the holds of the lease-lend ships and given to what were initially described as Home Guard Special Units. Some of these weapons are still in private hands, usually hidden in attics and gradually rusting away.

Then came the Sten gun, an invention which was cheap to make and designed mainly for distribution among the Home Guard, along with rifles such as Lee-Enfields. The official title was the Sten Machine Carbine Mark 2 and it could be fired using all types of 9-millimetre ammunition, including that used by the German army. This meant that captured ammunition could be fired back at the enemy. A large Sten gun factory was based in the Liverpool factory which in pre-war days produced the famous Meccano toys.

Many Home Guard units were very mobile and knew their own area well. There were units based on each large factory or mill and others made up of railwaymen, quarrymen and miners. These were distributed all over Yorkshire and literally were trained to look, duck and vanish. There were times, however, when it may have been necessary to fight from defensive positions.

Pillboxes

Pillboxes were not just erected anywhere but carefully sited at crossroads, close to bridges and in rings spread out from vulnerable coastal areas. The system and the design of these boxes were planned carefully and those which do remain should in my view be given the status of Grade II listed buildings.

In fact, no two pillboxes are alike because each was built to fit into the contours of the area and there were more than 30 different designs. Each was camouflaged, some to look like barns, hayricks or innocent dwellings. These days we see those which remain as stark oblong blocks of weathered concrete. What a good idea it would be to restore one or two properly and use them as a museum complex. I can think of ideal locations such as at Spurn Head or Kilnsea.

Reg King, now resident in the United States, agrees with me: 'At the start of the war I worked on constructing pillboxes all round the north-east coast. They were built of brick with struts of protective metal. Then they were covered in a thick layer of concrete. When we left them, the shell looked stark and easily seen but I later visited a few when the experts had converted them and it was almost impossible to find them as they were so well hidden in the landscape. Inside was sparse with the emphasis being on the machine gun mountings and the ammunition, but I'm told that the crews usually made them warm and comfortable and could get some sleep providing they did not mind resting their head on a box of bullets!'

The pillboxes were often occupied by a mix of regular troops with well-trained Home Guard men providing some relief, especially once the real threat of invasion had receded. What was essential was to protect vulnerable airfields and other installations from small-scale airborne attacks and the Allies followed this practice throughout the war. In the event, the Germans had too much on their plate to have time to implement such attacks, but nevertheless preparations had to be made.

Barrage balloons

Apart from pillboxes, wartime Britain, including Yorkshire, featured 'elephants in the sky', which was the friendly name for barrage balloons. One seven-year-old had another name for them – Flying Effluents!

Barrage balloons were there to prevent enemy aircraft from flying too low and thereby reducing the effect of bombings, but how useful they were can only be speculated upon. There is no doubt that barrage balloons floating over the centres of towns and cities were a real comfort to those below. The viewers did not, however, expect a free circus display, but this is just what happened over Leeds on 15th May 1940. The event caused such amusement that it appeared in the national newspapers but because of the secrecy existing at that time the event was simply said to have taken place in a 'northern town'.

The balloon broke loose from its cables and drifted over Leeds, knocking chimneypots off houses as it went. Sirens sounded as an air raid was obviously imminent. As the balloon reached St James's

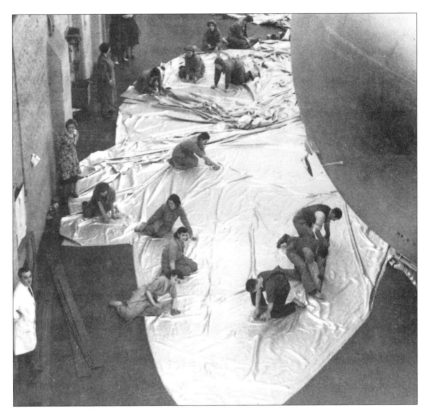

Some idea of the sheer size of a barrage balloon can be seen in this photo taken at the Dunlop factory in Manchester. The balloons were tested and inflated at the Bowlees factory, situated between Rochdale and Halifax.

Hospital a group of brave ARP men caught hold of a trailing wire and fastened it to a lamppost. The balloon had a mind of its own though – it uprooted the lamppost and continued on its rampages and was loose for around four hours. A troop of RAF men who were apparently used to dealing with escaped balloons finally secured the rampant beast on Sheepcar Street North but not before it had knocked down more chimneypots and guttering. A group of

35

boys from the Royal Park School followed the balloon and missed school. On the following morning they were given 1,000 lines to remind them that 'I must not follow barrage balloons'.

It may seem obvious that once hostilities were over, the balloons would be redundant and, on the whole, this was true. Marie Hartley, who wrote many books about Yorkshire, told me in the 1960s: 'In 1951 the BBC opened Holme Moss Transmission Station about eight miles to the south of Huddersfield. It is 1,720 ft above sea level near the summit of the Woodhead Pass. To see if the station was viable, BBC engineers carried out tests with equipment carried on barrage balloons. This work was done from 1947 onwards and the decision to build Holme Moss was taken in 1949, the main transmission mast for television and VHF radio, the latter having been developed during the war. For a while it was thought that the station was a secret listening device despite BBC publicity suggesting that it was quite the reverse.'

Barrage balloons were huge structures. When inflated they were 66 ft long, 30 ft high and needed 20,000 cubic ft of hydrogen, a most dangerous gas, by the time they took to the air. They could rise to 6,000 ft and were secured by wires attached to mobile winches. In view of this the miracle is that so few broke loose and ran amok. Each balloon was covered in valves, panels, scoops, fins and cables. Each cost £100 to construct and £25 to inflate.

The barrage balloons which hovered over the Yorkshire towns were tested at Bowlees. This is now an industrial estate situated just off the present M62 on the road from Halifax and Rochdale towards Manchester. The huge hangars where the balloons were once tested are still in situ and very impressive they look. They are now part of an industrial and retail complex.

The ARP and Police

While most of the activities of the Air Raid Precautions and their associated wardens will be covered in Chapter 3, which deals with Yorkshire in the Blitz, some attention must be given here to the development of this essential service.

In 1938 the Home Secretary asked for volunteers to 'assist with

Air Raid Precautions'. As with the Home Guard, the response was immediate and impressive. By 1939, some 1.5 million people were registered as wardens but what is far too seldom mentioned is that a quarter of them were women. All wardens were organised from a secure underground control room and had to fill in a secret report after each period of duty. As previously mentioned, wardens could refer to a booklet explaining their role but they had to buy it themselves, even if it only cost one penny. Neither were the ARP wardens paid for this service to their country. Andy Carter served for a time as an ARP warden in Hull during 1940 and said, 'I did not mind paying a penny and I think I know why this was done. You had to fill in a form to get the publication and so they had a record of who had the information.'

The wardens knew all the vulnerable sites and so did the Luftwaffe, so it is no wonder that wardens were vigilant and their 'put that light out' shouts were essential. Andy Carter continued: 'I loved the training we were given in First Aid and the value of keeping careful notes. We also had access to new scientific developments. I was told of the uses of a mineral called rock asphalt. This was proved to limit the impact of German incendiary bombs. Experiments in Switzerland had shown that asphalt does not burn and if masonry falls the asphalt smothers the flames. They also developed an anti-gas asphalt and included in our instructions how to deal with this menace. We were also told that reinforced concrete was useful in shelters as it soaks up moisture and helped to keep the damp shelters a little bit drier. We knew the position of some requisitioned private cars which were converted into auxiliary ambulances and kept in large buildings including dockside warehouses and in West Yorkshire wool warehouses.'

Andy Carter also told me that the ARP members and others involved in the Civil Defence were initially convinced that poison gas would be used. In the event, however, neither side used these chemical weapons but the threat was always there. Gas centres were set up in each town and great use was made of chemistry-trained schoolmasters in these centres. One warning signal consisted of painted boards which changed colour when they came in contact with gas. Decontamination centres were set up and thousands of gas masks were issued.

Mention here must be made of the strain on the police and how well they coped. The pressure placed upon policemen of all ranks at this time brought them almost – but thankfully not quite – to breaking point. It was here that the role of Special Constables was a vital one during the war years. I always feel sorry for the Specials – they had to pay for their own uniform, risk their own lives especially in the Blitz and were paid guess what? Nowt!

A Government publication of 1939 entitled *National Service* gave firm directions with regard to the duties of the Specials. Candidates were to be men of at least 20 years of age, of sound physique and health, as well as being of good character. Out-of-pocket expenses could be paid but this was the exception rather than the rule. Applicants were invited to apply to any police station. Yet more paperwork was generated as those wishing to volunteer had to complete Form Ed 60 entitled 'Form of Application for National Service'. There were regular and very thorough checks to ensure that all people engaged on official business had no criminal record and had what was described as a patriotic outlook.

Barbara Kirkland, who now lives in Whitby, remembers her maternal grandfather's role in the war: 'When the war started, the old fella had been retired from the police force for nearly ten years. At that time the police recruited members of the First Police Reserve and Police War Reserve. This was meant to attract retired officers and again they were not paid unless conditions became hazardous, in which case they would be provided with some brass. He took this position seriously and was in the heat of the action as bombs fell upon Sheffield. At this time he had to liaise with the ARP, ambulance service and help the fire brigades.'

Barbara Kirkland was right to put an 's' at the end of fire brigade. These days we are well used to our national fire service supplemented by some auxiliaries. Then, though, there was chaos in areas under pressure because each brigade had its own equipment and the fittings used by one brigade seldom matched those used in other towns. These problems were highlighted by Stan

Hook, who was a member of the Auxiliary Fire Service and who operated a motorcycle. In the event of radio or telephone failures, young Stan was to carry messages from one town's brigade to another in order to ensure that all fixtures and fittings were available. If there were no possible links, then there was no point in making the journey. The problems became really serious as German bombs began to fall and all services especially the Fire Services came under real pressure.

Stan Hook in 1940.

Chapter 3

Stop the Home Fires Burning

Britain was well aware that bombing of civilian targets would be a prelude to any invasion. To some extent the phrase 'Forewarned is forearmed' held true, but many people still believed in Neville Chamberlain's words 'Peace in our time' as he waved a flimsy piece of paper signed by Hitler himself at Munich.

Fortunately not everyone was so gullible, and this was the case in Leeds where Hitler caused a major rethink prior to war being declared. The city council intended to build a 23-storey skyscraper and planning permission was passed on 8th March 1938. The point was soon made, however, that the threat of war was so real that such a building would be a perfect bombing target. Plans were shelved and the proposed site is now occupied by Marks and Spencer.

The authorities in Rotherham were even more certain that bombing was inevitable and early in 1939 they anticipated the Blitz by removing the East window of All Saints parish church, which was hidden away deep in a local coalmine for safekeeping. This window is now back in its original position; called the

Te Deum, it was designed by the renowned Victorian architect Sir Gilbert Scott.

These two events – and no doubt many more other instances in Yorkshire – clearly indicated the expectation that Britain would be bombed and that Civil Defence strategies had to be planned in detail. Bombing of civilians, even if the aim is to reduce the industrial capacity, was always and will continue to be a contentious issue.

In 2007 I talked to Russell Margerison, who flew many sorties in Lancaster bombers over the German cities. I feel a bit sad because the bomber lads have been vilified for the casualties we inflicted and the damage caused to German towns and cities but it has to be remembered that the Luftwaffe had been the first to carry out a policy of saturation attacks with heavy bombers upon 'enemy centres'. During their blitz of our cities 43,000 civilians were killed, including around 5,000 children; on top of that 50,000 people and 4,000 children were maimed. Many more innocent civilians lost their homes, their pubs and their places of work.

Russell told me: 'Let's be fair, all war is bloody nasty and no one side should be blamed for air raids. One thing which is a fact is that the police and ARP wardens were told to keep accurate casualties a secret and bomb damage was labelled as 'in a northern town' rather than specifically referring to a named area. One of my best friends was killed in his Lancaster over Dresden in 1944 but he had already lost his wife and three kids in the bombing of Sheffield in December 1940. To say that he was bitter and determined to get his own back was the understatement of that or any other year.'

In March 1941 the Germans began to concentrate their blitz on the ports of Britain and on 8th March, as well as on the 7th and 8th May, Hull took a terrible pounding. Gwen Oakland of Doncaster recalled this when she spoke to Frank and Joan Shaw, who spent many years recording the memories of innocent people embroiled in the war. Gwen noted that, 'I was 9 years old at the time and lived in Hull. We spent many nights in our Anderson shelter and our dad was out most nights working as an air raid warden. He told us

The scene of devastation at Costello's Corner at the junction of Jameson and Sackville Street in Hull, May 1941.

Gwen Oakland (centre) as a young girl growing up in Hull, 1940.

nothing about his work and refused to talk about casualties – it was a secret. The shop where my dad worked in the daytime got bombed and he was moved to Doncaster which is where I live today.'

Horace Birkin remembers well the cloak of secrecy which surrounded Hull at that time: 'In 1940 I was L.A.C. in charge of a barrage balloon section close to Hull docks. When an air raid was due, we opened secret orders which told us at what height we had to fly our balloons – between 1,000 and 6,000 ft – and we had winches and more wire than you could shake a stick at. No doubt the varying height was so that the Germans could not predict where they would be. I don't think that people at the time ever realised just how much protection the balloons did give. This did not stop the blitz

L.A.C. Horace Birkin was based in Hull in 1940–41.

doing lots of damage and killing lots of people. I remember coming off leave and arriving in an air raid; I helped the local Civil Defence people to dig out a family but they were all dead including the children. I was told at the time to go back to my billet and say nowt. I said nowt but I had more than one tear in my eye. Later I was posted to the Bowlees barrage balloon factory at Middleton, between Rochdale and Manchester. I'll never forget that night in Hull when fires raged out of control and it was so hot that tar melted on the roads and tram lines buckled.'

Looking for survivors in Hull, May 1941.

It was not just Hull which had to endure a Yorkshire blitz, both Sheffield and Leeds took a horrendous pounding. Jim Roberts remembers one particular problem which in retrospect, as we have seen, should certainly have been anticipated:

'I was in the RAF at the time stationed at Biggin Hill and I was a fireman. I was in Sheffield when the bombing started and soon there were fires everywhere, mostly totally out of control. It was close to the centre but there seemed to be a real shortage of water. The problem was with the engines and it was here that the blanket of secrecy suffocated thought. Fire appliances were commandeered from all over South Yorkshire and the equipment and destination were known to only a few. What they did not realise was that in those days the equipment varied in size. When the trouble started it was suddenly found that the connections on the appliances did not fit the water mains and so the engines and their crews were bloody useless. I cannot repeat to you the language used by many brave and efficient firemen who felt so powerless and had to watch the city burn.'

Jim, even though he was in his RAF corporal's uniform, was warned off by what he called an 'ARP Hitler' as he got close to an area where there was an unexploded bomb: 'The team of Royal Engineers were much more friendly as they helped to control the two eager bystanders but I must be fair and say that the Royal Engineers and the ARP lads had a duty to protect the public and they had to prepare damage and casualty report forms which were on the Official Secrets Act. They did not want the public to know that 37,000 people had been made homeless in Sheffield, never mind those who had been killed!'

Elsie Probert told me: 'My father told me of a funny incident during the Sheffield Blitz. He never spoke of the civilian deaths and injuries but he told me the story of a cat up a tree. After the bombing he noticed a cat's eyes glistening in the light of a fire. The poor creature was terrified and mewing. My dad were, to say the least, a portly fella but he climbed up to reach the moggy. In doing so he got his trousers tangled in the branches of the tree. The cat looked at him and got down the tree as easy as winking. When

Bomb damage in Leeds, 1940.

daylight came the firemen got him down from the tree and he laughed about this until the day he died.'

Events like this – and there were many – show that the ARP men were not the tyrants which they have so long been labelled. It was therefore quite wrong to interpret all ARP wardens as 'Hitlers' or to believe the caricature painted in the comedy TV series *Dad's Army*. The wardens had one of the hardest jobs of all. They had to go into the heart of the bomb alleys created in most British towns and cities, as well as identify and count the dead plus writing down details of all important buildings which had been destroyed or damaged. At the end of a shift they had to sit down and fill in the official forms. When they arrived home the Official Secrets Act meant that they had to keep silent about what they had seen.

The morning after the night before – Sheffield High Street, December 1940.

'God bless our Anderson shelter', Leeds 1940.

In 1940 and 1941 the wardens based in Leeds had to be constantly alert and even those men telling people to 'put that light out' in the city of York suddenly had the war thrust upon them when the historic place was bombed and the medieval Guildhall was destroyed.

What is often forgotten is that in a blitz the normal telephone links were frequently severed. The fire service reacted in a sensible manner and some form of cooperation evolved even though the equipment from one area to another was often not compatible. Such a problem has already been described in the last chapter by Stan Hook, who now lives in Canterbury.

ARP wardens who had their own motorcycles were regarded as a valuable asset, as Malcolm Hall still clearly remembers although he is 96 and lives near Blackpool: 'When I were interviewed to become an ARP warden I knew I was wanted because I had a Royal Enfield motorbike and sidecar. Petrol coupons were issued and I could claim back the money but the machine could only be used when I was on duty. When the bombing was going on in Sheffield, I was used like a mobile office and moved from one post to another when the telephone lines were down. For a few days I have never worked so hard in my life. My bike had its paintwork scorched by heat and covered in dust and bits of burnt wood. In the sidecar I had a bucket of sand and at times it were needed. We worked closely with the police, fire service and even with the bomb disposal squad and I made many friends during these literally heated exchanges.'

The brave work done by these people should be recorded and one memory I shall treasure comes from Barrie Philips, who is now earning his living as a fisherman living close to Brisbane in Australia: 'My wife's father was a policeman in Hull during the war and he told us later that the number of fatalities during the blitz were kept secret. He also told us that the Germans had our equivalent of what he called "Dirty Tricks Boffins". Among the normal bombs, they dropped devices such as "butterfly bombs" which had rotating blades like helicopters and were coloured to attract children. They exploded when touched. They also dropped what we called "oil bombs". As you were working with the ARP chaps to clear up the rubble you came across what looked like a patch of oil which seemed to have melted in the heat. As you shovelled the bugger up it exploded. We learned to recognise 'em and reported them to the bomb disposal lads. Our reports were not, and still have not, been officially released. A lot of our reports and those of the ARP chaps were placed on a secret list and I was also told to keep quiet about an ARP post which had been knocked about more than a bit.

'I'll tell you one more thing before we go fishing and that was a rumour which went around the dock area of Hull. Very little bomb damage was done to a couple of the docks out of the eleven. Local folk still believe that the Germans were so sure of winning that they wanted to preserve an area which they could use as a U-boat base.'

Whilst this cannot, I think, be proved, I would not be surprised because in the course of researching this book I came into contact with many people who were sure that what went on in the area around Hull docks was one of the real secrets of the world war with rumours of spies everywhere. Notices to beware of speaking to strangers were displayed all over the docks.

Jack Carson, who still lives near Hull, has vivid memories of this period: 'I was nine when war started and my father worked in the offices at Hull docks. His brother had a similar job in the docks at Liverpool. I remember in April 1941 that my father had to go to Liverpool and he had a briefcase which he chained to his wrist and was full of papers. They were pink and had "Secret" stamped on them. He had a car with its army driver and I was allowed to go with him although I expect it was unofficial. We stayed overnight and my aunt took me to the pictures along with my cousin Geoff. Before we went we played "spies" in the garden, which was funny because the film we saw at the Forum in Lime Street was called *The Man Who Talked Too Much*. Neither of our fathers did that because they said "nowt". The month after the blitz started, Geoffrey's house was blown up and he was injured but recovered. He came to stay with us until they got a house and in that cold winter we played in the snow. Children at war, I think, were much

The Liverpool Forum where Jack Carson saw the film
The Man Who Talked Too Much *in 1941.*

more resilient than the adults and we enjoyed each day as it came with never a thought for the morrow.'

Some historians have tended to dismiss the recollections of young people as 'flights of childhood fancy' but this is a great mistake. These memories are as worthy of inclusion as those of older folk, who are just as liable to embroider the truth. What I found in the course of speaking to or reading the writings of those Yorkshire folk who were in the thick of it is that there was always much more truth than fiction in each and every account.

Documentary information is available but it has to be diligently searched for. In the case of this book I have had lots of willing assistance from reference librarians. The City of Sheffield, for example, published a *Where to Go* booklet issued by the Air Raid Precautions Department. This gave advice with regard to places to go when people were made homeless after a bombing raid. The local Home Guard units had a vital role to play and it is not often realised that many joined what was called the Women's Home Defence Force. These ladies provided a back-up service for the male members of the Home Guard. Sheila Ford has vivid memories of this period in Sheffield and I spoke to her at her retirement home in the Lake District: 'I alus laugh when it is said that we supported the men. Many of us were better organised and some of the fellas were so bloody useless that they could not open a tin. Many of us were more adept with regard to codes and signals and we became part of that secret war. I was just about to go to university to read French and German at Manchester when the war started. I became a part-time teacher helping to organise evacuations but also enlisted in the Women's Home Defence. Before that I signed the Official Secrets Act and was told to play dumb and look out for strangers with funny accents. I was to contact the nearest official – usually a policeman – and then shout out a warning in German to see how the suspect reacted. I often wonder what would have happened if I had had cause to employ this order.'

It was Sheila who put me in touch with Edie Benson. This fascinating young-at-heart lady was born in Normandy on Christmas Day 1900. Her ambition, she told me with a wicked grin, was to die on Christmas Day 2000. Alas she did not quite make it, but I spoke to her in November 1996 just before she died. In a lovely mix of French and broad Yorkshire she told me: 'Before I was married to an Englishman I was called Edie Solange and all my family for several generations had been fishermen around the coast of Normandy. From a child I knew the coastline very well and where I got it from I do not know but I could draw before I could write. By 1925 I was earning a good living as a painter and many British tourists bought my work. Then in 1930 I sold first one and then several paintings to Malcolm Benson. I still wonder if he thought it cheaper to marry me but I consented and in 1932 we married and I came to live in Huddersfield.

'Malcolm was a successful designer of textile machinery, especially in the woollen industry but also in the production of silk. When the war came I volunteered to help and then came a big surprise. They learned that I was an artist and I was asked to sign what I think was the Official Secrets Act. I was then set to work drawing maps, not on paper but on silk. I later discovered that these maps could be folded up without making a crackling noise and became part of a secret agent's equipment, and were also issued to pilots who might be shot down and try to get back home without being captured.

'In early 1942 the authorities wanted to see all my pictures of the Normandy beaches. They asked to look at all of them because they wished to conceal the actual area where the invasion was to take place. Later I discovered that other artists living in England were also contacted, especially those who had worked around the Calais area. They did manage to persuade Hitler that the invasion force could be concentrated around Calais rather than Normandy.

'From the end of the war until my husband died in 1981 we spent our summer holidays in Normandy and I paid our expenses plus some extras by painting "then and now" scenes with one side depicting Normandy before the war and the other showing the invasion beaches. Despite what you hear to the contrary, the French people are grateful to their island neighbours for their liberation and I am happy that I made a small contribution.'

It is memories like this which make the compiling of books such as these so exciting and I am thankful that I have kept a detailed diary since I was eleven years old. This allows texts such as this to breathe but there are times when it is essential to pore over archives and this could not be done without the help of reference librarians. I am particularly grateful to Michel Le Fevre in the Leeds Library who pointed me in the direction of mountains of well-documented material. I have made full use of this treasure trove of written information.

The first thing that Michel unearthed was a folder of huge maps of the Leeds area. These were not of local origin but were aerial photographs taken by the German Luftwaffe. Marked on these maps were the flight paths and bombing targets of strategic sites. One of those clearly marked was Kirkstall Forge, on the outskirts of Leeds.

Just before the outbreak of war Kirkstall Forge was easily converted into an armaments factory. As men were called up, they were replaced by women. Eileen Sykes who lived in Stanningley told me: 'After working in a mill I was sent to work in the munitions factory at Kirkstall Forge. I remember really long hours, I would go to work in the dark and come home in the dark. As well as working I also did fire duty at night. I was there during the bombing at Kirkstall Forge in August 1942. I remember watching the flares coming down. We weren't allowed to go into the same shelter as the men and so I had to run a long way. I got hit in the head with a piece of shrapnel but luckily I wasn't badly injured. Six men were killed in those bombings, it was a terrible night.'

Dorothy Titchmarsh of Horsforth, near Leeds, recalls: 'The Forge was bombed one night and quite a few people were killed. I was at home poorly on that night but we all turned up for work on the night after the bombing.' The fact that places like Kirkstall Forge

Eileen Sykes, who worked at Kirkstall Forge during the war.

An inflatable emergency water tank in use. These tanks came in useful either when the mains failed or when fittings were not compatible.

were targeted proves beyond all doubt that from the mid-1930s onwards the Germans had spies active all over Britain. As mentioned earlier Leeds Library has copies of Ordnance Survey maps marked up in German with all possible munitions sites carefully indicated.

Michel Le Fevre showed me a copy of a publication released in 1981 and which was entitled *Leeds at War* but surprisingly very few copies were actually printed. Many cities and districts including Leeds have kept their 'Emergency Committee Reports' which were obviously initially on the secret list but which were later bound into reference books. I was allowed to spend some time studying these reports. The City of Leeds has also preserved and produced bound copies of the Air Raid Precautions and Civil Defence Reports (1936–1945) and these are obviously also important reference points for historians.

Here are listed the locations of reservoirs and the relay links between the dams and points of delivery, as well as the locations of water mains and the emergency supplies. There were comprehensive lists of fire appliances and fittings. Even if these were not compatible between one region and another there was reliable data to indicate this fact. Private water sources associated with mills and factories were listed and mapped. There was a network of food and rest centres and all the Home Guard's 'normal duties' were listed, as well as instructions associated with the disruption caused by bombing. One interesting entry is under the title of 'Obstruction of Lights', which is obviously red tape jargon for 'Put that bloody light out'.

In connection with the Blitz are documents that relate to the construction of air raid shelters. Among the extensive and well kept archives of Leeds Library there is a photograph of a shelter built by Mr and Mrs Horace Fawcett in Cardigan Avenue, Burley. What they did was to strengthen their coal cellar and to furnish it in great style.

In contrast, the public shelters were more of a publicity stunt and were of little use. It seems fairly certain that they were not as safe as domestic shelters due to their poor construction – they were not heated and were very liable to flooding. Many shelters were large enough to shelter thousands of people and it would seem that to have so many people huddled together in one place was not a good idea, although it did give the ARP and rescue services an idea of where people were. Inside, the shelters were divided into rough dormitories and had bunk beds but there were no toilet facilities. After the war was over, most shelters were demolished but many Morrison shelters served as domestic tables and Andersons became garden sheds.

In addition to having to read reams of detailed instructions, all those involved in Civil Defence, as well as all workers and those who frequented pubs and other public places, were constantly told to be on the lookout for spies. It was particularly difficult in the ports such as Hull and Goole, as well as across the Humber to Grimsby in Lincolnshire. The problem there was that lots of Norwegians and Danes had decided to run the gauntlet of the North Sea and sail vessels of all sizes, from those with a crew of

'Life goes on' – celebrating Christmas in an Anderson shelter.

four to the large trawlers and merchant ships, to a haven called Britain. Most had at best a limited knowledge of English and spoke with a 'German twang'.

I spoke at some length to Charlotte Brownlow, née Nielsen, and she told me: 'I was eleven years old in 1939 and all of us in Denmark knew that the Germans were on the march and would trample through our little country on their way to plunder the rich iron ore deposits and deep sheltered harbours of Norway. I was surprised at the time when my mother and father held a party for their friends. There were Danish flags everywhere and we seemed to be eating up everything in sight. My father was a fisherman and my mother worked in the fish market on the Gammel Strand in Copenhagen.

'For the first time that I could remember I was taken with my mother to wave the trawler off. Suddenly we were bundled onto the gangplank, our outdoor clothing appeared as if by magic and off we sailed to I personally knew not where. We had a bit of a lumpy trip but we eventually docked in Hull and our trawler, which was a modern one, was renamed and became part of the British fleet. The same thing happened to others of our ships and we were joined by large numbers of Norwegian vessels. All this was done in great secrecy. After the war my parents went back to Denmark and my father continued fishing and mother stood the market. By that time I had an English boyfriend and I later married Alec Brownlow so I never went home. I did marry in Denmark and we still take our family holidays there. I expect there will be lots of other Danes and Norwegians who will want to share their secrets with you.'

This was indeed the case and I was contacted by Tomas Ericson, another Dane who spent the rest of his life in the Hull area until he died in 2007. Tomas told me: 'When the war was threatening I was working in the shipyard of Burmeister and Wain and I had only just qualified. As a young man who had Jewish relatives I knew that I had to escape. A friend of mine was a fisherman and over a drink we decided to take the risk and head off in a very small boat in the general direction of Britain. Eventually we landed in Bridlington harbour and I reported to the authorities there. At first

Gammel Strand in Copenhagen – many of the fishwives working here escaped to England with their husbands and settled in Hull.

63

A Danish steel trawler (left) and an older wooden trawler at Esberg shipyard preparing to leave for Hull.

the police were very suspicious but I was passed on to a military-looking chap with what I now know was an Oxford accent. He was followed by a Danish chap and another grilling before I was issued with an identity card and ration books. I was taken to Hull on a Friday night and given some digs; on Monday morning I was trying to understand Yorkshire humour and accent but my shipbuilding skills in a trawler yard soon made me welcome. I worked on the conversion of trawlers to minesweepers and it felt like home as I was first working on a couple of old wooden Danish trawlers.'

I remember Tomas, whose accent was a delightful mixture of Danish and broad Tyke. He supported Hull Kingston Rovers

Rugby League team and it was in this context that I met him. He also had a deep knowledge of Yorkshire cricket and the rules of the game. It is no wonder that he eventually remained here, married a girl from Goole and his grandchildren often still refer to him as a 'Great Dane'.

Fighting back

Did Britain have a voice to compete with the Nazi-lover William Joyce, also known as Lord Haw Haw? Indeed it did and broadcasts from London echoed all around the world spitting out defiance. This was not done in a BBC accent or with Churchillian oratory but in a broad Tyke accent. The voice was that of the Yorkshireman

Tomas Ericson, a Danish shipbuilder who escaped to England during the war and lived in Hull until he died in 2007.

J.B. Priestley (1894–1984). This monarch of English literature was born in Bradford, first worked in the office of a woollen mill and kept his accent to the day he died. His wartime broadcasts, called 'Britain Speaks', were transmitted all through the war from 1940. It has been suggested that in most of these rallying talks, secret code words were included and used by those working underground in occupied Europe.

One other man with a Yorkshire connection was a man called Ernest Shackleton. He graduated from Leeds University, obtained a post with GEC and was part of an organisation which later became a member of the Institute of Electrical Engineers. He joined the army at the outbreak of war and Captain Shackleton was captured in France in June 1940 and held at various POW camps in Germany. In September 1943 he was in Stalag IXa in Rotenburg.

The camp had an ancient, non-functional movie projector. Shackleton over a period pinched various valves and capacitors and wrapped some wiring round the cases of toilet rolls. This contraption became an efficient radio set and was hidden under the floorboards. Contacts were made by small holes into the floorboards through which knitting needles were attached to the set. Careful wiring of the set connected it to the mains without the Germans knowing. The radio was thus constantly on but no sound came until connected to the listening devices. These Shackleton constructed from toothbrush handles, which were insulators, and earphones made from cocoa tins and bits from a clinical thermometer. Radio Leeds would have been proud to have employed such a skilled radio engineer who knew how to keep his secrets to himself.

It was not just individuals who knew how to keep secrets but workers all over Yorkshire were prepared to work hard and say nowt – or at least next to nowt. Official visits of dignitaries were not reported until they had been and gone and even then the event was recorded but the precise location not revealed until after the war.

In order to keep up morale, public figures including the King and Queen and Winston Churchill toured the towns and cities and looked cheerful. Their meetings were kept secret until the very last minute for security reasons. On 5th July 1941 the Foreign Secretary Anthony Eden visited Leeds, arriving by air, having some lunch in the Civic Hall and addressing a crowd of 10,000 at Elland Road, the home ground of Leeds United.

On 6th February 1942 the French General Charles de Gaulle visited Leeds to celebrate what was called Allies Day. He announced that the people of Leeds had raised the staggering sum of £2,134, 287 to go towards the cost of the new aircraft carrier, HMS *Ark Royal*.

It is only when you look at such huge sums of money being donated that you realise just how much the civilian population contributed to the war effort and how vital it was for the morale of the people to be maintained.

Chapter 4

Eat Your Greens and Make Do and Mend

These days we take supermarkets and a plentiful supply of food for granted. You hear people complaining if they have to wait for a few moments at a busy checkout. Folk whose memories are very much part of this book were forced to queue often for hours on end to collect their meagre rations. As a child at this time I believed that the German larders were full of goodies. In fact, they suffered as well and at one stage even potatoes were rationed in Germany, which was never the case in Britain.

The authorities in Britain were well prepared and ration books were issued from October 1939 although the system did not begin until the cold January of 1940. The delay was due to a campaign mounted by the *Daily Express* which had the banner headline: 'Stop Rationing'. This was a stupid campaign which in retrospect was nothing short of criminal.

It may have helped if people in the UK had known that by 1943 the German rations for the week (above) were quite similar.

The production of the ration books and later the monitoring of coupons provided employment for many women and each town and city had a 'ration book room' which was a hive of activity.

When you take a look at the meagre rations which were considered adequate, the amazing thing is just how healthy people were at that time. Next time you go shopping, why don't you weigh out 12 ounces of sugar, 4 ounces of butter, 4 ounces of bacon, 2 ounces of flour and an egg? Then weigh out half a pound of meat and two sausages. No, this is not for your daily intake but had to last you for a week. Those who were fat in those days were naturally fat because there was no danger of over-eating!

These days we often see ration books illustrated in black and white rather than in colour. Hazel Bayliffe recalls: 'My first real job was sorting out ration books in Leeds. This was not so straightforward as most of us thought. We first had to check the

Women of Leeds preparing the first ration books, which were ready by September 1939.

Greta Gunson.

forms to see who was eligible, where they lived and how old they were. There were ration books of different colours. There was a green book issued to pregnant women and children under five. This meant that they could go to the front of the queue and also be given fruit if there was any available. They could also have two eggs each week plus one extra pint of milk. Children between five and 16 were issued with a blue ration book and could have an extra pint of milk but only if and when supplies allowed this to happen. The rest of the population were given a buff-coloured book. The books contained coupons which were cut out as rations were issued. Each person was told which of the registered shops they had to use.'

Greta Gunson takes up the story: 'My dad was manager of a Co-op shop in Barnsley. His job was to sort out the coupons and send them off to a registered office where they were scrutinised. I remember him telling me years after the war was over just how carefully these coupons were checked and he and his staff had to be able to recognise the customers on their register.'

Barbara Middleton also had to go through this routine in her first job which was in a draper's shop in Halifax: 'Everybody talks about food rationing but few people realise that the same applied to clothes. People would save up their coupons for weeks just to buy a dress or a pair of trousers. What the fashion-conscious youngsters would think of this today I shudder to think.'

Apart from rationed goods, most other items, especially cigarettes and beer, were very often in short supply. What shouldn't be forgotten is that at this period of history women were very much second class citizens. When the war started in 1939 ladies had had the vote for only about 20 years. Furthermore, smoking in public and drinking in pubs were mainly activities for men and usually the only females who entered this

Cigarettes were available but it wasn't always possible to obtain any preferred brand.

male preserve were prostitutes. In this context the suggestion that only men should be allowed to buy cigarettes is less ridiculous than it seems to us today.

Maud Jobson, now in her nineties and living in Whitby, told me: 'The war did two things – it got rid of Hitler and it gave women more freedom. We were no longer confined to our homes and shops as had been the case with our mothers but there was a real need for us to go out to work. If we were doing a man's job, we also demanded his degree of freedom. I started to enjoy the odd fag and I still do at my age. I worked packing shells on the outskirts of Bradford, I wore make up and sometimes went to the pub with my boyfriend, who became my husband for more than 50 years.'

Reg Parker, and it must be said many of his young friends, welcomed this change: 'You should remember that in them days almost every man smoked and if you went to the pictures you saw the show through a thick mist of smoke and the whole place smelled of it. Even though tobacco had to be imported no government could ever have contemplated fighting a war without fags.'

The same thing applied to beer, and the breweries which are still famous in Yorkshire to this day were working at full capacity in an effort to keep up with demand. Tetleys and Theakstons have never been so popular and that is saying something. The only time pubs were in trouble was when they ran out of beer. This did occasionally happen when demand outstripped supply, perhaps when large numbers of troops were stationed in areas of low native population. Men fought in pubs not because they were drunk but because they wished they were! This was certainly the situation in the Saddleworth area. Colin Mills told me: 'When the Americans came into our little villages like Dobcross, Delph and Diggle – which sound like a firm of Dickensian solicitors – they soon learned to drink warm Yorkshire ale. The problem was that they drank too much of it which upset the local lads. Not only was there beer brewing but so was trouble.'

In the end, however, things settled down and the Yanks were on the whole welcomed, especially by the children who were given comics, cookies and gum. Anyone who gets the chance should see a re-run of the film *Yanks* which was filmed in Saddleworth. Obviously the film makers romanticised and built in stress and strains but on the whole it gives a fair impression of Yorkshire at war.

Prior to the start of the war and rationing, it was already obvious to everybody that Britain did not grow enough of its own basic foods and was importing far too much. To some extent today the economic crisis of the past few years has led to a 'grow your own' culture and there is a great demand for allotments. Early in the war 'Dig for Victory' posters were everywhere and everyone, even town dwellers, was encouraged to make use of every bit of land.

Sheila Parker remembers this time well: 'We had a small garden in our house on the outskirts of Skipton. We had no indoor toilet but a privy at the back and this was joined by our Anderson shelter. My dad was away in the army but my grandad piled up earth over the tin roof of the shelter and over the privy. This provided enough soil for us to grow cabbages, leeks, carrots, cauliflowers and Brussels sprouts. Grandad let me have a small garden of my own and I still love growing onions and potatoes. We kept rabbits but I learned to keep away from them because I got upset when they finished up with the carrots in a pot.'

Alan Bowker remembers his schooldays near Harrogate: 'We had our own allotment and there was also one on the edge of the school playing field. There were colourful posters put up in school giving names to vegetables. I remember Potato Pete and I can still recall the verse which was printed at the bottom of the publication. It went something like this:

> *Here is the chap who ploughs the fields*
> *Here is the lass who lifts up the yield*
> *Here is the chap who deals with the clamp*
> *So millions of teeth can chew and champ*
> *That's the story and here's the star*
> *Potato Pete*
> *Eat up, Eat up*
> *Ta Ta! Ta Ta!*

'We also had Doctor Carrot who helped us to see in the dark and it would seem that there was more than a grain of truth in this. Carrots are rich in sugar and when grated and used in cakes they saved the precious sugar ration. Parsnips had even more sugar in them and our teachers invented Percy Parsnip and we drew our own pictures of him. Later when television came, Percy Thrower had a gardening programme and in our family we always called him Percy Parsnip!'

It was not just individuals who were Green for Victory but the farmers also had a vital role to play. At first they did not like to be

73

told what to plant and in what quantities but most soon realised that this interference made sense. With young men being conscripted for the army, it was soon clear that there was going to be a serious shortage of labour. The answer was obvious – bring in the ladies and call them the Land Army.

It is too often said that the Women's Land Army was formed in 1939 but actually it goes back to the First World War and 1917, before women had the vote and when ladies flexed their muscles to help to grow more food when shipping losses were restricting supplies. Now, thousands answered the call and by 1944 there were 80,000 women digging, ploughing and planting for Victory. On the whole the scheme worked well and relations between the farmer and the lasses were good.

There were, however, a few exceptions as Doris Denver remembers very well: 'In 1939 I was about to leave school and had got the offer of a job as a weaver in a woollen mill in Bradford. I was not all that keen because I had seen my mother coming home so tired that we all had to set to and make tea. We heard a rumour that war was certain and that our mill was to be changed into a factory making shells. It was then that I saw an advert for the Land Army where all lasses like me could work on farms and spend the period of the war in the open air. Seven of us from Bradford were sent to Cheshire and given some, but not a lot of training. Three of us were given our uniforms including the green pullover and armband. We were billeted in the barn of a farm near Bridlington and I'm not mentioning the farmer's name in case his family are still alive.

'The best that I can say about him is that he was a foul-mouthed bully who was eventually caught for fiddling his books. His farm was repossessed which happened a lot in the war. To begin with I was called 'D.D.' but because we got so mucky in wet weather I was Dirty Doris and we also had Mucky Mary and Boggy Beryl. I won't tell you what Sylvia was called! None of us minded because it was all in good fun. I had some wonderful times and I never expected to be involved in secret work but it came about like this.

'One day it was still dark when we were picked up early in the morning but this did not matter because the bus windows were blacked out anyway. Inside was a policewoman and an old chap with a clipboard who ticked off our names. He carried a map with a lot of red dots on it and which looked like a twisted chain. We were told to say we had been given a free day out in Scarborough; he gave us a packed meal and told us to say nowt. We were then driven around pillboxes which were so overgrown that the line of fire of the defenders was obscured. We trimmed the branches and wove them into camouflage netting and then we were blacked out again and only the chap with the maps knew where to go next. As we worked, old motorcycles kept whizzing past and never used the road once. We did as we were told and said nowt but we were all convinced that the Nazis were coming.'

It is amazing how the little pieces of a jigsaw which is Yorkshire's secret war fit together. The motorbikes scrambling about the pillboxes must have been part of John Warburton's communications network.

George Simms told me of one unusual aspect of the Land Army: 'In 1942 I was working as a farm labourer near Pickering and we were soon joined by girls from the Land Army. One girl – Michelle Latour – was French and she and her mother escaped to England before the war started. Michelle's family were farmers in the Loire Valley and her father was shot whilst working for the Resistance and so were her two brothers. After the war we married and it was only then that I discovered that Michelle had inherited not just a farm but also a sizeable vineyard. I'm nearly 90 now and I look forward to English folks like you buying my wine and getting my Yorkshire accent back on line!'

He then produced a case of wine, winked at me and said, 'Nah then, lad – thee take that 'ome and gerrit supped.'

The last word on Yorkshire's 'Dig for Victory' should go to Alec Dukes. He was 93 when I interviewed him in 2001: 'I were one of a lot of Yorkshire fellas who dug not once for victory but twice. I did my shift down a coal mine and then spent some time on my allotment. Most miners felt claustrophobic down the

George Simms, a Tyke, became a vineyard owner in France after the war.

dark 'ole so we wanted to get out in the open air as soon as we could and fer as lang as we could. Miners are a tough lot, especially my mates in Barnsley, and the spivs knew to keep well away from us. There were miners with big fists and our dogs had bloody sharp teeth!'

There is no doubt that both the Dig for Victory campaign and the Women's Land Army worked well but there were potential disruptions to the food supply chain. One very secret aspect which I had never come across before was the proposed decontamination service, set up to deal with food which had been contaminated by gas. Initially in Leeds there were 66 staff but this later increased to 171. Each individual was provided with protective clothing and aspirators issued by the Ministry of Home Security, and there were also extra items which were deemed necessary to protect those in contact with contaminated food. The site selected to deal with the food was called the Decontamination Station and provided by the Health Department. Adjoining was an office and equipment store controlled by the Food Decontamination Officer. This was J.A. Dixon, but he had a deputy who had an even more imposing title and doubled as the Chief Sanitary Inspector.

The members of the service were given training and then organised in squads controlled by a leader. Leeds developed methods which were said to be groundbreaking and used as a blueprint for the rest of the country.

In the event this extensive and expansive scheme never had to be put into full operation. What did cause massive disruption and what is not a proud period in our history, however, concerned the black market. The portrait of 'spivs' was but the tip of the iceberg and many more innocent-looking characters made a good if illicit living out of the hard-working, law-abiding citizens.

Not only were there large-scale, well-organised gangs rustling sheep and cattle, but there were smaller operators who came out of the cities and raided the countryside. One such gang was described to me by Ian Heavyside, who became a teacher of chemistry in Beverley. He told me with a huge grin on his face: 'My maternal

A gas-powered police car. Many vehicles, including buses, were adapted to run on town gas contained in huge balloon-like structures on the roof.

father-in-law had an allotment near the old church at Bingley and he kept having his vegetables pinched by a gang, probably from Leeds, and he found out who some of them were. He was a retired chemist and one evening he dosed some cauliflowers with a strong laxative. He watched them steal these whilst sitting in his garden hut. He said later that he helped to keep the Black Market running!'

Some gangs were small-scale and may have stolen for their own consumption – let us hope that this was the case with the Bingley theft – but there was a huge earner for those prepared to take the risk. A lucrative crime was to syphon off fuel from parked vehicles, especially buses and even army wagons. Lots of stealing went on, too, particularly during air raids. Cigarettes were another target and many thieves broke into ration stores so Home Guard units were deployed to guard these valuable supplies.

There were also raids on farms and I know of one wartime thief who still walks with a limp because he was caught in the act of 'rustling' two pigs by three farm labourers near Ripon.

Village people looked after each other and they would band together to 'look after intruders'. Most had what they called 'pig clubs' and whilst most animals were licensed there were 'unofficial' pigs which were kept away from prying eyes. Slaughter took place in secret places and each member of the club got their cut. In the days before refrigeration, food could not be kept and so those in 'pig clubs' had a list of which animal was next 'for the chop', if you will forgive the pun!

In the cold snowy winters of 1940 and 1941 with no central heating and houses warmed only by coal, there was a shortage of fuel. The problem was not the output from the mines but transporting the coal in bulk because of the weather. At this time there was pilfering from the coal dumps of the woollen mills and especially from railway yards. Home Guard units were recruited from the railwaymen themselves and their first job was to protect the lines, as well as the infrastructure of the depots. Once the invasion threat had diminished the Home Guard patrolled to prevent pilfering from the locomotive tenders.

Providing food and the fuel to cook it on was a constant challenge and the logistics of rationing meant that shift workers and those working extended hours needed to be fed. The government was well aware that rationing would not be popular and that people at work, especially if they had some distance to travel, would not be able to provide themselves with a substantial packed lunch, which in any case would eat up far too much of the family rations. The authorities were also aware that cafés would be inclined to charge what they wanted and thus the better off would be better fed. From 1942 onwards the maximum price for a two-course meal was set at five shillings. Even then this was beyond the means of most people.

The Home Office therefore provided funds to allow large factories to set up their own canteens. Sheila Brady recalls: 'I worked in a woollen mill in Batley and until the war we had to rush home for our dinner or else sit by the loom and eat while you soaked up some much needed energy. We had to work harder in the war and had paid overtime which was a luxury after the problems of having no work at all through most of the 1930s. Then we had our own canteen where we could get a basic but hot meal and be warmed by a huge black pot-shaped boiler. This were luxury which only people who lived through this period can ever appreciate. I spent nearly six years weaving a blue cloth which was used to make airforce uniforms.'

Even more central government funds were provided to set up what became known as British Restaurants. Some of these were created in town halls whilst others were purpose-built, usually from corrugated iron and concrete. The roofs rattled when it rained and many were cold in winter, but at least the food was hot and, on the whole, edible and above all it was cheap. One such purpose-built restaurant was on Kirkstall Road in Leeds and within walking distance of Headingley cricket and rugby league grounds. The price of a two-course meal was set at only ninepence. There was a careful scrutiny of identity cards to ensure that no person could have second helpings. The serving utensils were each of an exact size so that all helpings were the same.

With the Dig for Victory campaign in full swing there was a surfeit of vegetables at certain seasons and those who grew their own could sell their crops to the British Restaurants. Any scraps from the kitchens were sent to the locals who were raising pigs. This also applied to the school kitchens. The largest schools had their own kitchens whilst meals for the smaller schools were sent from a central kitchen and kept hot in large churns surrounded by bales of straw. Schoolchildren were also provided with a third of a pint of milk presented in a bottle with a straw. I well remember on cold winter days the milk bottles being left on top of radiators, which was in most of our opinions the wrong option. We would have preferred cold milk rather than drink it 'lumpy' warm and almost sour. This was in the days before semi-skimmed milk had been 'invented' and it was all full cream and not far removed from the dairy cows!

*A British Restaurant under construction in Kirkstall Road,
Leeds during the war.*

One item of diet which is now becoming so expensive that it is
classed as a luxury is fish and chips. In the war, although most
trawlers were requisitioned by the Admiralty for minesweepers,
some old slow vessels were brought out of retirement. With no
refrigerators, fresh fish had to be delivered and eaten quickly. Fish
was only rationed by supply but most fish and chip shops remained
open at least on two or three days per week. Two of the largest
fishing ports were on opposite sides of the Humber – Grimsby on

the Lincolnshire side and Hull on the Yorkshire bank. Both were served by a network of railway connections and a fleet of lorries. The latter went to the towns whilst the fish vans were provided with enough petrol to enable them to deliver to country districts where queues would gather around the Hull fish vans.

Like everything else, in these relatively peaceful and easy times we take our transport systems for granted. The only time the railway network is mentioned is when normal service is disrupted. Few of us realise just how much pressure the railway system was under during the war and how well it coped, nor how difficult it was to move goods by road before the days of the motorway!

Chapter 5

Transport under Pressure

At the onset of war, Yorkshire had three transport systems which were very loosely interlinked but still largely independent. These were rail, canal and road. As with all industrialised counties, the transport system was more comprehensive than in other areas that had less of a manufacturing base. Even then, however, Yorkshire was an exception. Mainly because it was by far the largest of the English counties, it was regionalised, with the industrial bases being in the west and the south. Here there were the coalmines and the mills, with the docks and fishing port around Hull having developed an impressive industrial infrastructure. These transport systems were well known to the Germans and the Luftwaffe had very detailed maps of potential targets, as described in a previous chapter.

Railwaymen at War

In 1939 there were four railway companies operating in Britain. These were the Great Western Railway (GWR), the Southern Railway (SR), the London, Midland and Scottish (LMS) and the

London and North Eastern Railway (LNER), the latter being the most important so far as Yorkshire was concerned.

These four companies were only formed in 1923, when the problems faced during the First World War were analysed and acted on: how could troops and goods be moved when there were upwards of 50 railway companies all with different rolling stocks and timetables and stations which were largely independent of each other? At the onset of the Second World War, however, each of the quartet was taken over by the government in order to co-ordinate the supply of food, troops and other vital raw materials. There was thus a single nationalised system in operation. The railwaymen were told to keep destinations and the goods they were carrying very secret indeed.

There were two main lines; the first between London and Glasgow, a West Coast line with servicing yards at Crewe and Carnforth, and the second the East Coast route from London to Edinburgh via Doncaster and York. If bombing raids ruptured one of these lines then there was one link between the two which thus became vital and it seems that the Germans were never aware of its importance. This was the 76-mile line linking Settle and Carlisle. Completed in 1876 by the Midland Railway, it had been a nightmare to engineer and was a difficult line to operate, especially in the winter but it was a sheer delight in the summer.

I had many long conversations with Bill Donley, who was a close friend of my late father-in-law: 'I was a signalman and trained in Leeds but in the war I spent some time as a signalman at Dent, which was the highest station in Britain and was more than two miles uphill from the little village itself. I was told of the strategic importance as a line which connected the West Coast and East Coast routes and sworn to secrecy with regard to what materials and weapons were on the goods wagons, and told not to talk to the troops on passenger trains if they stopped for any reason. During the winters of 1940 and 1941 the snowstorms blocked the lines and troops and railway workers used shovels, sometimes with no effect at all, to release trapped engines. I still laugh about when I was told that even the weather conditions were secret!'

The engine pulling this train was built in 1944 by R. Stephenson and Hawthorn. It is rushing past the Skipton rock quarry that was kept hard at work providing materials for the bomb-damaged cities of Leeds and Hull.

In a strange way this did make sense because a stationary train is much easier to hit with a bomb than is the case with a fast-moving train.

Bill Jenks takes up the story: 'I would leave home in the early morning at Doncaster and only when I met up with my fireman who was getting steam-up was I told where I was going, but not always what I was carrying. The drivers' footplates in them days were open to the elements but the boiler fire usually kept us warm and dry. Then came the war and it was realised that as we opened the boiler door to add coal the light at night could be visible to planes high above. What they did was to enclose the cab in thick light-proof tarpaulins. This was quite cosy in winter but in summer it was as hot as hell and we lost pounds in sweat. We were all experienced railwaymen and we knew which stations we were passing through even though all the names were painted out to confuse enemy spies. The mindset in those days was that it made sense to assume that every stranger we met were a spy. If it was a chap, we would ask him questions about the Yorkshire Rugby League teams and that went some way to sorting things out.'

Even though the station names were painted out, there were posters everywhere telling folk that 'Tittle tattle lost the battle' and asking 'Is your journey really necessary?'. Other colourful posters persuaded young women to join the Land Army or take a job in a factory – and as we have seen, everybody was told to 'Dig for Victory'.

Bill Donley remembered this time very clearly: 'Just before the war there was a continuing tradition that the porters on each station kept a garden and there were prizes awarded to the best. It very much resembled the Best Kept Village awards which we have today. In 1939 the names of stations were painted over and the lines of flowers which picked out the name were grubbed up. Flowers were replaced by cauliflowers and climbing roses were joined by stands of peas. Dig for Victory was also a feature around some of the big stations. Every bit of spare land was used and at least this was one aspect of the railways at war which did not need to be kept secret!'

*Railway signalman Bill Donley (right) with the
author's father-in-law, Wilf Jaques.*

The massive movement of people and materials put immense strain not only upon the lines and the essential maintenance involved in repairs and replacements but also on the locomotives themselves. As the men who built and serviced these vast machines were called up, it meant firstly that retired workmen were called into service. When this was not enough then the answer was obvious – bring in the ladies, and history shows what an efficient job they made of it.

From the beginning, as already briefly mentioned, many railwaymen were drafted into special Home Guard units as they obviously had a greater understanding of how to protect a rail network and its production sites. I interviewed Alec McIntyre who told me: 'I came from Glasgow in 1924 as an apprentice in the huge locomotive works at Doncaster. I was drafted into the Home Guard and those of us who knew how to keep a railway running also knew how to stop it running should the Germans land in Britain.'

Others like Len Townsend were given, according to his daughter Margaret who lives near Doncaster, 'secret orders of how to wreck trains and uproot tracks in the event of an invasion. This was only part of his work in the war as he had spent his working life helping to build some of the world's finest and fastest steam locomotives, including the *Flying Scotsman* which thankfully has now been restored to its finest glory.'

Many steam railways operating today for tourists and enthusiasts pay special attention to the often traumatic events of the Second World War and have weekends devoted to the subject. Serious enthusiasts dress up in period costume and uniforms and those interested in this period of history should not miss attending one of these events.

Yorkshire has three such steam railways. The North Yorkshire Railway is based around Goathland (telephone: 01751 472 508). The railway line was closed during the Beeching cuts of the 1960s and had been engineered by George Stevenson in 1836. It opened as a tourist attraction on 1st May 1973. Visitors should never be afraid to ask questions because all staff on these lines are volunteers and have a passionate interest in the history of the line, the locomotives and the rolling stock. In any context, but especially during the war, the supply of functional wagons was just as important as the locomotives which pulled them.

I have spent many happy hours talking with Stephen Walker, who is the manager of the Embsay and Bolton Abbey Steam Railway (telephone: 01756 794727). When I asked Stephen about railways in the Second World War his eyes lit up as he said, 'All the railway network was in full swing at that time – new locomotives were being built as fast as possible and old stock restored and kept running. We have tried in our stations at Embsay and Bolton Abbey to give the restaurants the feel of that period and open coal fires are a real feature. The food is not of that vintage, however. We have regular Second World War weekends but perhaps even more relevant from the point of view of the book you are writing is our collection of photographs. Some of our volunteers have memories of this period.'

One of the drivers was Keith Emmett who remembers when he was a schoolboy seeing goods wagons being pulled by two engines and '... although they were covered in tarpaulins we could see guns and tanks on them. This was in 1944. Obviously in the build-up to the Normandy invasions the line became stretched to its capacity and beyond. None of the railwaymen knew where their loads were initially heading and orders often came in the middle of the journey.'

Even more facts await visitors to the Keighley and Worth Valley Steam Railway (telephone 01535 645214), which became famous for the setting of the first and so-successful film of *The Railway Children*. Scenes from the film *Yanks*, already mentioned, were also filmed on this line.

During the war, Keighley and the area around it was of great importance because the town had long earned its living by producing some of the finest heavy textile machines in the world. With such engineering expertise making up its workforce, it is easy to see how these skills could be adapted to serve the war effort. The railway route which follows the Aire Valley was a vital link to Lancashire in one direction and the Yorkshire towns and cities in

*This locomotive, part of the Embsay and Bolton Abbey Steam Railway, is a
saddle-tank engine built in 1939 by Hudswell Clarke*

the other. The main line is still operational into Yorkshire but the infamous Beeching cuts of the 1960s caused more disruption than the Luftwaffe. Thankfully, the Worth Valley line which runs from Keighley into Haworth and the villages beyond can still remind us of the war.

Also in this context, a visit to the National Railway Museum at York (telephone: 08448 153139) is a must. Visitors to the archive are made most welcome, as I discovered when I met Tim Proctor and other archivists in this wonderful purpose-built complex, with its panoramic window overlooking an exhibition room. Visitors should be happy to accept the rules which apply: the only equipment which can be brought in is a notebook and pencil, and bags must be placed in secure lockers outside the room. Sadly, experience has shown that, in the past, archive material has been stolen or defaced. Security here is tight enough to remind us of the blanket wrapped around sensitive material during the war.

Here is the place to study the archives of the Doncaster Locomotive Works and also a smaller works based at Hunslet where shunting locomotives were built. Rolling-stock works can also be traced. This linked in to a discussion I had with Olive Huddleston who told me: 'My family were involved with railway locomotives from 1873 and my father and uncles worked at Doncaster and at Hunslet. I'm ever so glad that part of the latter works situated close to the Rugby League ground is now used by the Middleton railway near Leeds as a tourist attraction and involves a display of the old works dating from the 1860s. You should not miss this little gem. My grandad worked on building some of the world's most famous engines at Doncaster, and actually Sir Nigel Gressley who designed so many of these steaming monsters was based at Doncaster. My dad and two of his brothers were engine drivers so one generation built 'em and the next operated 'em.'

George Openshaw worked at Doncaster during the war and later in the works at Crewe, where he still lives, now retired and in his early nineties. He told me, 'I noticed a major change as war loomed. Before this we clocked in at work but later we were checked in and out and our identity papers were scrutinised. We also had to work under much more pressure and had to keep old locomotives running which in peacetime would have been scrapped.'

All local people referred to the Doncaster works as 'The Plant' and it was established by the Great Northern Railway Company in 1853. The Plant was world famous in the 1930s for constructing locomotives which could reach speeds of 100 mph. On 3rd July 1938 the *Mallard* achieved the world record for a steam locomotive of 126 miles per hour.

During the Second World War, The Plant also produced Horsa gliders which played a vital role in the Normandy landings. The works was high on the Luftwaffe's 'hit list' but the only major damage during the war was to the carriage building shops, which were destroyed by fire – but not due to enemy action – in 1940. The site was only 'destroyed' in 2008 and has now been replaced by housing. It is a shame that such an important part of our heritage has disappeared. Surely there should have been some room left for the construction of a Heritage Centre.

Historians should be ever grateful that the National Railway Museum has scrapped nothing. One collection which I thought at first would be of little interest were the huge piles of posters relating to the railway period. As I flicked through those from the Second World War, I realised what a treasure trove of history was being revealed.

As early as August 1939 the following notice was posted around all stations throughout Britain:

The railway companies regret that in consequence of the crisis it is necessary for them to give notice that their regular passenger and goods train and boat services may be considerably curtailed or interrupted and they will only be able to book passengers and accept traffic as circumstances permit, and then only on the understanding that they cannot be responsible for any delay, damage or loss which may arise through any such curtailment or interruption.

This was a valiant effort of the new railway set-up to cover all eventualities, but a further notice was published as the summer holidays approached in 1940 and the Yorkshire resorts were torn between repelling a potential invasion from the sea and yet trying to raise revenue from the usual influx of visitors. Two notices appeared on all stations:

There isn't even half an engine to spare for unnecessary journeys. Stay put this summer.

Later in the war came this plea:

Holiday trains in short supply.
The reasons:
Shortage of labour for repair of coaches and
engines worn out and damaged in war service.
Passenger coaches may have been sent overseas.

In 1944 a publication was prepared by the Press Office, then located within Waterloo station, entitled *British Railways in Peace and War*. This was on sale at the price of one shilling and printed in the poor quality paper typical of the period. Obviously the supply of wood pulp from such places as Norway, Sweden and Canada was very much restricted. The statistics quoted in the publication make fascinating reading. By the end of 1942, for example, the lines of track stretched for 1,265 million miles and engines ran 1,870 million miles. The strain on the goods system was tremendous. In addition, 30,000 million miles had been travelled by troops and passengers. This demand built up to an even greater extent following the Normandy invasion by the Allies.

All railway movements were kept very secret and the company gave each journey a code, a combination of letters and numbers which indicated the route. Journey times, numbers of troops carried and the armaments they needed all had a reference number. This worked so well that the enemy did not expect the North African invasion despite the fact that 1,150 freight trains were all allocated a port, a berth and a specific ship. There was an organised system of control rooms all over the country.

A similar timetabling system was in operation to cope with the mass movement of evacuees. In the event of an invasion there were detailed timetables to evacuate entire towns and even large cities such as York, Hull, Leeds and Sheffield.

The issue of how to react to air raids was also the subject of careful planning. Again, with the communications system at that time restricted, there was no way to relay information electronically and therefore railway staff had to be carefully briefed and notices placed in prominent positions. The LNER railway had a well tried system. A preliminary warning of an imminent raid was the display of a large orange sign and the local ARP were told that once the trains had stopped passengers had to be directed to the nearest shelters. A red sign indicated that bombing was in progress – as if folk did not know – and a green sign meant 'raiders passed'. ARP wardens and station staff then directed passengers back to their trains.

Edith Philpott remembers this period well: 'I was passing through Doncaster on my way to take on my first job, which was at the aircraft factory at Yeadon, when the train stopped. Porters opened the doors and ARP and police hurried us down to the shelters. All this was done in the dark which for a young lass was scary. There I bumped into Mary Gillbanks, also on her way to Yeadon, and we have been friends ever since; we both met our future husbands at the factory and so I never went back home to Maidstone. Soon wardens shouted "Green light" and we resumed our journey after about an hour. You know you have to have lived through the blackout to know just how difficult it actually was.'

A Road Without Lights

Derek Chalmers of Rotherham told me: 'During the war my mother, who was a big strong lass, drove heavy lorries to and from the Hull docks. She always tells the tale of her father who drove a steam engine and she said he had it easy in the blackout because all he had to do was follow the track. In contrast those on the then narrow roads had to drive with headlights dimmer than dim and with their bumpers and running boards painted white. Even the policemen on duty wore white coats and were locally called "ice cream merchants", especially if they had a bike. There were continued calls to the bobbies to "Stop me and buy one"!'

With such restrictions on lighting the accident rates did increase and gave the authorities some cause for concern. On the whole, however, it was decided that these increased risks were worth the price. At least in those days there were fewer vehicles on the road and, in any case, petrol was rationed. Buses, like trains, carried notices pointing out that short distances should be walked to leave room for those travelling longer distances to get to work. One rhyme was relevant at the time read:

> *He's only got a step to go*
> *A couple of hundred yards or so*
> *While others further down the queue*
> *Have far to go and lots to do.*
>
> *When George gets on we often find*
> *That other folk get left behind.*
> *He pays his fare and rides the stage*
> *And off he hops to see the rage*
> *And seeing this gives George a jog*
> *'Perhaps I'm just a transport hog?'*

All buses and trains had blinds on their windows and these were also covered with strips of paper. This patterning was called scrim and was to prevent windows shattering due to a bomb blast.

Often we do not realise how important the network of canals were which criss-crossed Yorkshire. To list all of them would be tedious but there were navigations between Leeds and Liverpool, the Calder and Dutch Navigations around Goole and the Rochdale Canal which ran from Manchester to Sowerby Bridge.

Jane Middleton, who now lives in retirement in Morecambe, told me: 'Lots of retired Yorkshire folk live in Morecambe and at one time it were called Bradford-by-the-sea. During the war we lived near Castleford and my grandfather worked on the coal barges. Folk don't realise these days just how much traffic was carried by canals and neither do they know how much cheaper it was. Grandad crewed a barge which trailed behind it a lot of containers full of coal. Many of these were loaded from chutes very close to the pitheads. They were piled high and had such a shape that we called them Tom Puddings. Grandad not only worked on his barge but lived on it. It were reet warm in winter and obviously he always had a coal fire to keep the family warm and had a stove attached so that they could cook their food. My father and his three sisters were born on the barge. I remember him telling me that between the pits and the power stations there were lots of lovely countryside and he were keen on wildlife until the day he died. As a family we often spent our holidays on canal boats which must have been more luxurious than in grandad's day.'

Power stations were obviously vital during the war and were guarded by units of the Home Guard. They kept potential saboteurs at bay but were not safe from bombing. Contingency plans were put in place, as was the case in these beleaguered times, as Gordon McInnes recalls. He was 93 when I interviewed him in 2004: 'During the war I worked for the Ferranti Company based in Manchester and I helped to make what are best called mobile power stations. They were diesel driven and could be transported in railway and even canal containers, as well as by road. When vital supply lines were broken, power could be restored in a matter of minutes.'

As we've seen in this chapter, all transport systems had to withstand enormous pressures. Despite 'Digging for Victory' and 'Waste Not Want Not' campaigns, Britain was still dependent upon imported food. This had to be brought in by sea and this is the subject of the next chapter.

Chapter 6

War at Sea

I n 1939 Winston Churchill, then only First Lord of the Admiralty and not yet Prime Minister, launched Operation Fish. This simply meant extending a First World War scheme to requisition any wooden vessels, but especially trawlers, to serve as minesweepers and escort vessels. They needed trained crews and many trawlermen from Hull and a few from Whitby were drafted into what became known as the Royal Navy Patrol Service (RNPS), which was based in Lowestoft. The facility was set around an old theatre and became known as the Sparrow's Nest, with its trainees becoming part of the brave and resourceful 'Harry Tate's Navy'.

Some of the vessels requisitioned and brought into service, such as the *Windermere* and *Domino*, were ex-whalers sailing out of Whitby and Hull. The *Sierra* was a whaler built in 1929 and was regarded as an ideal minesweeper. Even a paddle steamer called the *Gracie Fields* was involved in keeping the channels free from magnetic mines.

All those involved paid a heavy price and by 1940 100 RNPS vessels had been lost. By the end of hostilities more than 2,000 vessels and 70,000 men were involved in this very underrated service.

Later, the so-called Fish Class vessels, such as the *Bream* which was launched in 1942, were purpose-built for minesweeping but afterwards became very successful fishing trawlers. There was still

At the beginning of the war, some trawlers were used as patrol ships. The officers' job was to board merchant ships and confiscate any goods which could be sent to help the German war effort. Here wolfram is being confiscated as this was used in the production of steel.

plenty of work to be done once hostilities had ended. Many vessels were employed in clearing up loose mines which for several years remained a problem as merchant ships started to ply the old trade routes.

A great deal of secret work went on apace from 1937 onwards as the Admiralty under Churchill followed a blueprint drawn up during the First World War. The idea was to requisition not just trawlers but also their crews, and place young naval officers in nominal charge. All aboard knew who was actually in charge, and that was the experienced fishing skipper. It was also essential to have an experienced radio operator trained in the latest techniques.

According to its age and condition, a trawler was put to work as a minesweeper, on anti-submarine patrol or as a fleet tender. Alec Gilham remembers these days as if it were yesterday. 'Me and my brother came from Lowestoft until we married girls from Hull in 1937. Both of us were crewmen on trawlers which were taken over by the Admiralty. We were skippered by a young brash naval officer but he were soon sorted out by our skipper who had been at sea for more than 30 years. We was at Dunkirk and this were bloody rough – don't be fooled by the passage of time – it was bloody rough. I'll tell you what annoyed us even more than being shot at and this was at first we were not allowed to fight back. Later on I were trained to use a Lewis gun and although it were nowt but a pop gun it made us all feel better. After the war my brother collected photographs which he intended to put into a book but he never got on with it. I still have some of his collection and you can borrow them if you like. He had one copy which is now in the Hull Museum of a ship called *Lady Lillian* and he had friends aboard her. In 1939 they changed her name to *Jade* as she was fitted up for anti-submarine duties.'

The *Jade* had an active war and Alec Gilham continued: 'One of our friends trained as a wireless operator and he was on duty patrolling off Malta when she was struck by bombs and had to be scrapped. Some of the crew were flown back to Blighty and were on other trawlers which saw service during the Normandy landings.'

*Eventually, but under a cloak of secrecy, trawlermen were trained to use a
Lewis gun and at last could fight back.*

Trawlers from Fleetwood, Grimsby and Hull were requisitioned by the Admiralty and were adapted for use as minesweepers, fleet tenders and also for patrol duties, armed with very modern radio equipment.

The Lady Lilian *seen here on her 1933 trials, complete with flags, was taken over by the Admiralty in 1939 and renamed* Jade.

Sheila Cooper also has a lasting memory of this as part of Yorkshire at War: 'My great uncle was a trawler engineer and we lived in Hull. I was about 10 and I remember him going to sea in 1939 to meet a chap called Harry Tate. It was only after the war that I realised that he had been conscripted into the Royal Naval Patrol Service and he told me that at first the trawlermen did not always get on very well with the young Navy lads who were only nominally in charge. There was a bone of contention in that the trawlermen were Merchant Navy and got no pension and no wages from the minute they were sunk. In contrast the Naval youngster was sure of a wage and a pension. My great uncle Dan grinned and said that all class distinction disappeared if bullets were being aimed at your arse.'

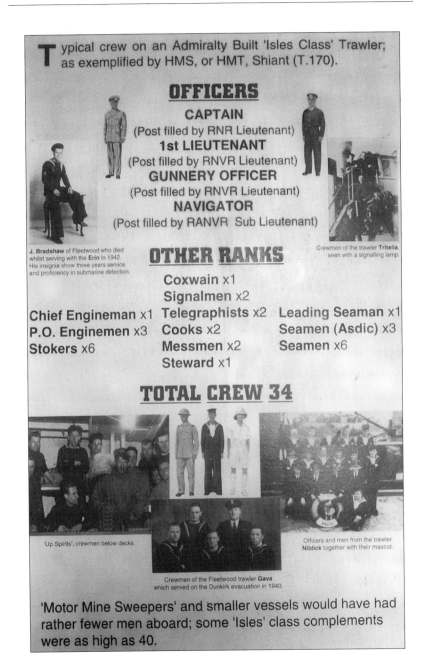

Typical crew on an Admiralty Built 'Isles Class' Trawler; as exemplified by HMS, or HMT, Shiant (T.170).

OFFICERS

CAPTAIN
(Post filled by RNR Lieutenant)
1st LIEUTENANT
(Post filled by RNVR Lieutenant)
GUNNERY OFFICER
(Post filled by RNVR Lieutenant)
NAVIGATOR
(Post filled by RANVR Sub Lieutenant)

J. Bradshaw of Fleetwood who died whilst serving with the Erin in 1942. His insignia show three years service and proficiency in submarine detection.

Crewmen of the trawler Tritelia, seen with a signalling lamp.

OTHER RANKS

Coxwain x1
Signalmen x2
Chief Engineman x1   Telegraphists x2   Leading Seaman x1
P.O. Enginemen x3   Cooks x2   Seamen (Asdic) x3
Stokers x6   Messmen x2   Seamen x6
Steward x1

TOTAL CREW 34

'Up Spirits', crewmen below decks.

Officers and men from the trawler Niblick together with their mascot.

Crewmen of the Fleetwood trawler Gava which served on the Dunkirk evacuation in 1940.

'Motor Mine Sweepers' and smaller vessels would have had rather fewer men aboard; some 'Isles' class complements were as high as 40.

Sparrow's Nest recruits at Lowestoft in Suffolk.

I have known fishermen and especially trawlermen for most of my life and they had three characteristics which were ideally suited to war conditions. Firstly, they learned quickly because those who did not got injured and a few suffered an even worse fate. Secondly, all trawlermen could keep secrets because no skipper or his regular crew would divulge the locations of their favourite fishing grounds. Thirdly, and perhaps even more importantly in war conditions, all men of the sea helped each other when danger threatened.

Minesweepers were vital because magnetic mines were creating absolute havoc. The Germans developed secret components inside, which triggered an explosion whenever a steel-hulled vessel passed close by. As trawlers had lots of wood in their hulls they were ideal vessels to serve as minesweepers.

Whenever there is any conflict there is always a battle between one set of scientific boffins and another, with each group of scientists hell bent on defeating the opposition. There is no doubt that in the early stages of the war the German scientists working on magnetic mines, especially on the triggering mechanisms, were way ahead.

The Admiralty in London funded lots of experiments but most proved to be totally ineffective. Fortunately for the British scientists, one solution almost literally dropped in their laps. A German seaplane offloaded two magnetic mines which fell on the mudflats of the Thames estuary and failed to explode. This dangerous duo was carefully defused and examined in great detail. It then took time for a defensive strategy to be evolved, but there was a great urgency in the trawler ports to have a reliable method of dealing with this lethal threat, which was causing such a debilitating drain on British exports from the sea. All coastal waters around Yorkshire and the Humber were being constantly mined and efficient minesweepers were urgently required.

Eventually a technique known as 'degaussing' was evolved, which meant passing an electric current through cables girdled around a vessel and literally neutralising its own magnetism. Then the vessel could pass a magnetic mine in relative safety, as Michael Kenny recalls: 'I was sixteen when the war started and I was

The armband worn by the Mine Clearance Service.

working with my father as a carpenter on the Hull docks. My stepmother owned a boarding house close by and we had four large rooms for let.

'Just as the war got under way a man came from the harbour authorities and booked all the rooms until further notice. Soon three very smart men arrived and they set up one room as an office. They journeyed to the docks every day carrying very heavy briefcases and one man spoke with a foreign accent. One day we were working on a trawler which had just come in from Fleetwood when these chaps came aboard carrying what looked like lumps of wire and a compass. They stayed aboard for three working days and hardly ever came "home". The man with the accent we later knew as Mr Olsen and he was always talking to the crewmen. We were told that these men were Danish and they had sailed their trawlers from their home port to prevent them being taken over by the Germans. At this time we realised that Mr Olsen was not actually a German spy! After the war George Olsen went back to Denmark but he came to us for his family holidays until the day he died in 1980. It turns out that George was an electronics expert who had been trained in Germany. He would never talk about his work in the war except to say that he was an expert degausser. He was always full of praise for the brave trawlermen who he said should have had more gallantry awards than they were given.'

There was a tradition of trawlermen being prepared to take great risks in the heat of battle. In the First World War after 32 Hull trawlers were sunk by mines the Admiralty reacted by forming the Mine Clearance Service and this was immediately reactivated as a second war became certain.

The minesweepers had the job of locating mines and marking their positions so that they could be disposed of in the safest possible way. Michael Kenny is certain that it was in this area of expertise that the three men located in his house were especially skilled.

Another problem which had to be solved was that once a ship was sunk by a mine in a position likely to block an important channel, it had to be blown to pieces on the sea bed or blasted clear of the channel and its position marked by a buoy. The Admiralty had a number of specially equipped Wreck Disposal Vessels based all around the coast, so that they could operate as quickly as possible. The usual method was to attach a series of charges on one side of the hull of the wreck. The explosion created a deep trench into which the wreckage was dropped. This was an expensive business and it has been proved that in some wrecks several hundred depth charges were needed to clear a blocked channel caused by the sinking of a large ship.

The day after I had spoken to Michael Kenny he rang me up to say that no account of Hull's secret war at sea would be complete without a mention of 'Mad' Rilatt who became a legend in the Naval Patrol Service.

Edward Spencer Rilatt was a taciturn character very active in both wars who, in 1926, bought shares in a Hull trawler called the *King Emperor* and set about creating a family tradition by encouraging his two sons to become trawlermen. Edward, his eldest son, was killed in action aboard the Hull trawler *Sedgefly* on 16th December 1939 but Ted battled on and was hell bent on revenge. He had shown his patriotism in the first war and had a reputation for his often fanatical bravery – his nickname 'Mad Ted'

Ted Rilatt, not 'Mad' Rilatt as his nickname suggests but a brave and efficient seaman.

was not an insult but a compliment and his seamanship was legendary.

Several incidents stand out and if ever an adventure film deserved to be made about a man of the sea then it should be based around the exploits of Ted Rilatt, who was not only awarded the MBE but was also the recipient of the much coveted French award, the *Croix de Guerre*. Had it not been for his short temper and often rightful indignation directed towards Royal Navy officers then the Honorary Commander of the Royal Naval Patrol Service would have been given the British wartime medal which he richly deserved.

One memorable incident was when Rilatt was the skipper of the First World War vintage trawler *Dawn*. She was sweeping mines along with other vessels when a U-boat surfaced and opened fire. Ted and his crew had been trained at Lowestoft and an accurate shot actually sank the U-boat. All the crew were complimented upon their fearless behaviour.

'Mad Ted' is really the wrong name – 'Master of Subterfuge' would have been a far better one. One event would have done credit to the Secret Service at its very best. Ted was operating his trawler clearing mines on the approaches to the vital port of Harwich. As fast as he cleared mines by day, the U-boats came in at night and laid more. Rilatt's ruse was to pretend to sweep mines but to actually leave them in position. This was done and the next morning a U-boat was found to have been sunk by a German mine! Not Mad but a Magician of Tactics!

Not so pleasing to the high-ranking officers at the Admiralty was the behaviour of this upstart captain of a 'minor boat'. Ted was on patrol between Scotland and Norway actually laying mines when a British destroyer was torpedoed. Ted began to rescue survivors and skilfully manoeuvred his Hull-based trawler *Pomona*. His crewmen were busy pulling men from the sea, including some French liaison officers, when a second British destroyer moved in. Her captain seemed to be more intent upon glory for himself and 'buzzed' Ted's trawler out of the way and almost certainly prevented some men from being rescued. The destroyer herself was then torpedoed and Ted's boys were once more pressed into action.

Charles Ayre on the Kitty. *He may not have been uniformed but he was very much a part of Yorkshire's secret war.*

There was still a great loss of life but the destroyer captain himself was rescued. When he landed safely he offered his hand to Ted who was 'mad' with rage and spat on the hand and taught this man a lesson in Anglo-Saxon with a Yorkshire accent!

There was a move afoot after this to court-martial Rilatt but the reports sent in by the French liaison officers nipped that in the bud as they were about to give him the *Croix de Guerre*! There is no doubt that Ted Rilatt's logs and tactics of minesweeping were copied in secret and used as blueprints for the correct way of dealing with the menace of mines.

Another gritty Yorkshireman who played a vital role in Yorkshire's war at sea was Charles Ayre. In 1983 I had the pleasure of interviewing Charles about his wartime work around the Humber. From the minute he opened his mouth his dry Yorkshire humour was apparent: 'When folk ask what my job was before I retired in 1973 I tell 'em I was a taxi-driver. This was not a lie but mine was not an ordinary taxi. I had a 39-ft motor launch called *Kitty*, expecting to attract tourists to enjoy pleasure trips during the summer. As events turned out I designed a much better business which operated all the year round. This boomed from the late 1920s with trawler owners who had new vessels going through their paces in the Humber estuary. I also did good business from late trawlermen who were ferried to ships which had sailed without them, and I was employed by postcard companies who sent photographers to produce pictures of the docks. The advantage of the *Kitty* is that she was small enough to get into each nook and cranny. In the mid to late 1930s large numbers of German marine engineers used my vessel as they were touting for work around both sides of the Humber. Why they needed so many cameras and notebooks in which they made sketches we now know. They all went back just before war was declared and if I had known what they were up to I would have dumped the buggers overboard.

'As soon as war was declared I had more and more work to do as trawlers were brought in to be converted to serve as minesweepers. They needed the help of pilots, especially in times of heavy weather or fog. The *Kitty* may have been small but she was

The Kitty, *with her open bridge, alongside the trawler* Lord Hailsham.
She was torpedoed by an E-boat in February 1943.

a good sea boat, as well as being a nippy vessel in and out of berths. Obviously it was kept secret but I was employed in the DEMS scheme which meant Defensively Equipped Merchant Ships. Seamen were ferried to a vessel on which anti-aircraft or anti-submarine guns were fitted. Once their accuracy had been assessed the marksmen – some of 'em certainly weren't marksmen – were returned to shore and the ships sent to sea equipped with their new toy. Another of my jobs which I did not like much was to sail around the estuary and the approach to the docks looking for mines, plotting their position and negotiating around them. I wanted to join the Navy but was told to shut up as I was already in it!'

From this chapter it is obvious that Yorkshire's contribution to the war at sea was largely one of defence, but no war is ever won by pure defence – only offensive operations can bring victory. In this sense, Yorkshire's contribution was immense and the county became a huge arsenal with tanks, shells and explosives being high on the agenda. It was in victory in the air where Yorkshire's contribution can be shown to be of great significance.

Chapter 7

War in the Air

Some years ago, I interviewed a chap called Stanley Jameson for a BBC radio programme. Stanley was then in his 87th year and he told me: 'All my life I have had two main interests which were finding out about aircraft flying at very high levels and playing golf at a very low level. I was living in Otley and had an ambition to play on each and every golf course in Yorkshire. I found one which will interest you because it played a valuable part in World War Two.

'As I started to go round the course at Howden, just off the present M62 and not far from Goole, I noticed the remnants of what seemed to be large hangars but no runway. I was told to go into the clubhouse and there on the walls were photographs and plans of airships. It turned out that in the 1920s and very early 1930s the British were trying to keep ahead of the Germans in the construction of Zeppelins to be used for both civilian and military purposes. In Britain there were two rival companies, one based at Cardington in Bedfordshire and the other the Vickers Company, first based in Barrow and then relocated to Howden. The chief designer of the R100 project was Barnes Wallis who later developed the 'bouncing bomb' which made the Dam Busters raid possible. He also designed the Wellington bomber using similar construction techniques and light alloys which he had perfected in his airships.

The R100 airship under construction.

Barnes Wallis had an invaluable assistant at Howden. This was Nevil Shute who later became a famous novelist. All production came to a grinding halt as the Cardington-built R101 airship crashed with many fatalities.'

When I was researching this present book I remembered my meeting with Stanley Jameson and visited the Howden site myself. There I was made aware of Nevil Shute's autobiography in which he was at pains to point out that the Barnes Wallis designs were radically different from those of the R101. There was, Shute

119

*Robert Blackburn (right) with his brothers Charles (left)
and Norman, photographed in 1928.*

pointed out, lots of secret work done at Howden which they did
not want the Germans to know about. New aluminium-based
alloys were being developed which were stronger and lighter than
others available at the time. Also secret was the geodetic
construction which later proved ideal in the development of
bombers. This lightweight solution led to the British having the
four-engined Lancasters whilst the Germans never developed a
four-engined aircraft because the airframe needed to carry them
was far too heavy.

This aspect of Yorkshire's secret war has never been mentioned
in any detail so far as I am aware. In fact, it was not until I began
to work seriously on this title with the emphasis on 'secret' that I
realised just how great a part of our aviation history took place in
Yorkshire.

The development of aviation in England's largest county was due
almost entirely to Robert Blackburn. His family was based in Leeds
and originally specialised in the manufacture of steam-driven road
rollers and other cumbersome vehicles, which resulted in the
making of a large fortune.

In 1908 young Robert was impressed by the achievements of
French aviators, led by Bleriot. The first Blackburn-inspired plane

A Blackburn Mercury monoplane on a test flight in 1911 on Filey beach.

The all secret, all metal, all action Blackburn Skua.

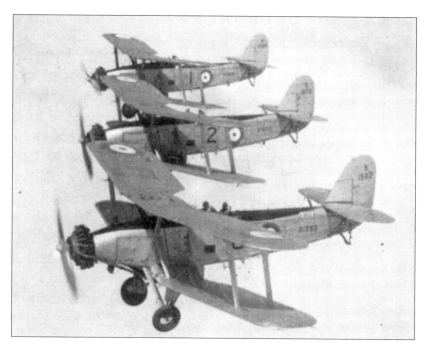

A formation of Baffins in 1935.

A Shark fitted with floats and, thus, a seaplane variant.

flew from Filey and a few other Yorkshire beaches from 1909 onwards and his off-shoot company soon developed a reputation. I subsequently met, corresponded with and spoke to, men who worked on Blackburn projects from the 1930s onwards. Their influence upon the war in the air was considerable.

Following those successes on Filey beach the company took over an old roller skating rink at Roundhay in Leeds. At this time the focus was on biplanes to function as torpedo bombers. These aircraft may have been slow but they were very manoeuvrable and from the late 1920s there were many German spies visiting the area, operating under the guise of 'fascinated tourists'. They were not just interested in the aircraft themselves but also in the bomb designs and the explosives and fuses within them.

The main prototypes which were tested around the Yorkshire coast were Ripons, Baffins, Sharks, Skuas, Rocs, Bothas and Firebrands. Edwina Jackson's father worked on several of these prototypes as an airframe fitter, especially on Baffins and Sharks:

'Dad told me that the idea that only monoplanes helped to win the war was not quite true. The biplane torpedo bombers and seaplanes built at Blackburn's did lots of damage to German vessels, especially U-boats. Another thing which made him laugh was the fact that many believed that the Blackburn company was based in Lancashire because of the name of the town. There is no doubt that Robert Blackburn was a Tyke to his fingertips.'

Leslie Jackson recalls working for Blackburn's from the mid-1930s: 'I worked mainly on the Shark and the Baffin, both of which had trade secrets built into them which we had to keep away not just from the prying eyes of the Germans but also of the rival companies in our own country in what was a competitive business.'

'Oh aye,' Eric Mulligan agreed, 'I remember working on the Baffin at the Brough works in 1933 and if I remember reet they used the same airframe to produce the Ripon. There were two variants which at the time were very secret. We knew to keep our traps shut because we did not want rival companies to pinch owt. One variation carried a huge torpedo which had a secret type of

Olympia Blackburn's works at Roundhay in 1915.

detonator which primed the weapon. The other variant had extra fuel tanks fitted and was an out and out bomber. The design of our airframes was more like a First War aeroplane and was soon replaced by the bigger monoplane bombers and which had nowt to do wi' us. It were the torpedo-carrying craft which were in use by the Fleet Air Arm all through the war. These machines had the advantage of being very manoeuvrable but were very slow. Both the Ripon and the Baffin which replaced it gave good service.'

I personally remember these aircraft whilst I was serving in the Royal Air Force in the mid-1950s. The hangars at Halfar air base on the island of Malta were demolished by a tornado which swept the island in December 1936, and the tale of which my Maltese friends related to me 20 years later. Those few Baffins which survived the onslaught were returned to Brough although regarded as obsolete. The design, however, was improved and renamed the Shark. Baffins, however, did see service during the war, operated by the New Zealand Air Force until 1943 or 1944 when the Japanese were a real threat to the area and surveillance of the sea lanes was of vital importance.

*Three photographs of Blackburn G.P. seaplane 1415 taken by
the company in 1916.*

It was at this time that I became interested in the history of combat aircraft and enjoyed hours of research whilst off duty. With me at that time was Derek Foulds, who later became a famous actor and John Pendlebury, who was a very skilled aerial photographer. This was the time when biplanes were still perceived as weapons of war.

The Shark, which replaced the Baffin, was well known to Edwina Jackson: 'I remember my dad talking about the Shark and in particular him talking about the weaponry they carried. I remember him drinking tea with his friend Sid Gregg in the 1970s and even then they seemed reluctant to talk about the secret bits even though they had been obsolete for years. You have, I think, to have lived through this stressful period to appreciate how vital it was to keep your mouth shut.'

What is interesting about the Shark is that its early prototype was called the TSR 1. People still wonder why the ill-fated TSR 2, which was cancelled in such controversial circumstances by Harold Wilson's government in the 1960s, was so named. How strange that a Yorkshire-designed aircraft was the original TSR 1 and that another Yorkshireman cancelled the supersonic TSR 2.

The Shark assembly line at Brough in 1935.

The Blackburn Design Team at Brough: Major F.A. Bumpus, designer, chief engineer and joint managing director (1919–1951) and Major J.D. Rennie, Seaplane engineer (1923–1946).

The TSR 1 was soon to become the Blackburn Shark. Its revolutionary design was its strengthened girder system and easily folded wings so that it could be employed on the flight deck of an aircraft carrier. There was also the then very secret hydraulic wing-locking device built by the Lockheed Hydraulic Brake Company of Leamington Spa. Deck handling and taxiing were also made easier by the fitting of pneumatic wheel brakes and what was termed a 'Tracking Tail Wheel'. These inventions were high on the secret list and those who fitted them into the airframe did not realise just how revolutionary they really were.

The Shark first flew in 1936 and continued in full active service until 1944. Some models were fitted with floats and given extra fuel tanks instead of armaments. The aircraft did wonderful service picking up survivors from sinking ships and shot-down aircraft. John Crossley was born in Hull and at the age of 19 in 1943 his merchant ship was sunk by a mine in the North Sea. He was picked up out of the water by an aircraft built near Hull.

He recalled: 'I remember helping to assemble Sharks and then one day some of us were told that we had been carefully selected to work on the assembly of an aircraft called the B24 and which was later named the Skua. We were taken into a blacked-out room and shown a huge diagram projected onto a screen on the wall. We all gasped because it did not have two sets of wings but only one. None of us had expected the company to take such a risky change in design policy. There was also to be

G.E. Petty, Blackburn's assistant designer 1918–1937, and then chief designer 1937–1951.

a fully enclosed cockpit. Then they put on the lights and pulled a tarpaulin off a huge engine which had 840 horsepower, made by the Bristol Engine Company. We were told just how secret this was – it was in late 1937 – and we looked again at the airframe and wondered how it would cope with such a bloody big engine. We need not have worried – it worked to perfection.'

The revolutionary design involved the construction of several fuel tanks and a method of transferring petrol from one tank to another which was invaluable if the aircraft ever suffered battle damage in such a vulnerable area. The Admiralty wanted Skuas for use as dive bombers and once the prototype had been agreed, 190 were ordered.

Eric Collinson, who now lives near Skipton, told me: 'I soon realised that the production targets for the Skua could not be fully met at Brough and parts were built at the Olympia works at Roundhay in Leeds and the Blackburn company sub-contracted some work to General Aircraft Limited at Hanworth. I was sent to both these places to help to train new workers. Many of these willing folk, including girls, had never worked on aircraft but they were used to working on or near the heavy machines used in woollen mills. They adapted well and with great speed. No sooner was one type developed than another came on line. When the war broke out, the Skua was tried and tested and they were soon on the flight decks of the *Furious* and *Ark Royal*. They provided invaluable protection for the battleships *Rodney* and *Nelson*.'

Colin Bickerstaff remembers that: 'I did not work at Brough for very long as I became a pilot flying Skuas, but I do remember Robert Blackburn himself visiting the shop floor and he had with him a pilot who was, I think, a Lieutenant Commander in the Fleet Air Arm. He told us how grateful he was to the workers who had kept quiet about the secret stuff incorporated into the Skua. He gave us a first-hand account of an action in which a Skua shot down a German Dornier flying boat off the coast of Norway. I volunteered to become a pilot the morning after his visit.'

The ill-fated Narvic Operation off Norway was a disaster in planning and many Skuas were lost during this engagement in 1940. Skuas, however, did have some successes, notably the sinking of the German battleship *Königsberg* close to Bergen harbour on 10th April 1940.

When I was working for the BBC in Norway during the summer of 1976 I came across Lars Admundson who told me that a team of divers had discovered the sunken wreckage of a Blackburn Skua: 'We all knew about the brave pilots who fought against the Germans at the time of Narvic and a Skua piloted by a man called Partridge had to force-land on a frozen lake. A few years ago lots of our divers went down and eventually recovered the aircraft and it was sent to a museum in England.'

Winston Churchill himself heard of the exploits of this aircraft and said, 'The Blackburn Skua contributed greatly to Britain's strife towards defence of its homeland and its ultimate aim of winning the war.'

I eventually located the wrecked Norwegian Skua at the Fleet Air Arm Museum at Yeovilton in Somerset where it is part of the Skua

Underwater Exhibition. I later wrote to Lars Admundson to tell him where the aircraft was and I had a fascinating and surprising reply: 'The Skua to us was, and still is, part of our very own secret war. It was the first and only combination of fighter and dive-bomber monoplane which the British used in the whole of the war. We also knew that it was the very first all-metal monoplane to be invented. It was also the first to have a retractable undercarriage.'

From this and other accounts which I have pieced together it is obvious that the Skua should be included in any account of a secret war and that the Blackburn company should be given a very honourable mention. It was also a Skua which was the first to shoot down a German aircraft in the Second World War. As mentioned above, they played a vital role in the sinking of the *Königsberg* and, later, Skuas were sent to attack the *Scharnhorst* in Trondheim harbour. This time the Luftwaffe were present in force and half the Skua squadron was lost. The Norwegian people remember the sacrifice made by these brave pilots and venerate the name of the Blackburn Skua.

As is the case in all wars, progress in the development of weapons was so quick that almost as soon as an aircraft was off the secret list it became obsolete. So it was that by late 1941 the Skuas were only retained to serve towing targets to allow air gunners to become more proficient.

The same story concerned the Blackburn B-25, soon named the Roc, which was prophetic as this prehistoric flying bird also became extinct! The Roc in its early stages, however, initially had a number of very secret innovations mostly relating to weapons release gear and variations in the retractable undercarriage. Blackburn had a contract for 136 aircraft which was signed on 28th April 1937. The company was hard pressed to deliver this order, as well as coping with orders for the Skua, and with the Botha set to become their latest model on the assembly line. By 1940 the Roc was being delivered but was already somewhat obsolete as more advanced models were evolving at great speed. Rocs, however, gave good service to the Fleet Air Arm until well into 1943.

Eric Morley told me: 'I loved working on the Roc even though I knew that its operational life was bound to be short. Every day the boffins seemed to be coming up with something new and we had posters all over the shop floor telling us that Hitler was hiding under the benches and listening to each and every word. One innovation in the Roc was that the fuselage was widened so that a power-driven gun turret could be fitted in. This was the first fighter with a revolving gun turret to be flown by the Fleet Air Arm. The two-man crew must have felt cramped – the pilot was sheltered from the weather beneath a sliding canopy, with his observer squeezed in behind. He had two jobs rolled into one. He had to operate the wireless apparatus and also be prepared to squeeze into a narrow alley leading to his new gun turret. This had two pairs of Browning .303 machine guns which could be fired by one electronic button. There was one further secret device which allowed the guns to rotate over 360° without shooting off the propeller. I'll bet the Jerries would have loved to get their hands on one of these devices. Whilst we were working on the Roc we were also beginning to assemble the B626, which was a different aircraft altogether. It had two engines and became known as the Botha, but we soon called it our "Bother Bus".'

Eric Mulligan's first job as a 16-year-old in 1939 was to train on the assembly line of the Botha at Brough: 'The first thing that I realised was how modern and sleek the Botha looked. I did not know at the time that there were so many top secret innovations within it, but these were soon replaced by more modern refinements. I still think that the "Bother Bus" would have been a winner if it had not been for one major drawback. This was the pair of Bristol Perseus engines, each of 850 horsepower. In retrospect it is certain that even these were underpowered for the airframe to handle. I know that the Blackburn bosses wanted to use Bristol Taurus engines, each of which had 1,150 horsepower and which would certainly have made the Botha more competitive. Had they used the Bristol Hercules engines, which were in excess of 1,500 horsepower, our "Bother Bus" would have caused the Germans much more bother than was the case.'

For those reasons the Botha should be regarded as a nearly-but-not-quite aircraft let down not by its design which had so many secret innovations but by the lack of the power sources which the planners had asked for. Nevertheless this aircraft filled a vital gap in the early years of the war and thousands of skilled men and women were kept hard at work at Brough, whilst at the Olympia factory in Leeds components were built in vast quantities.

The Botha was in production by December 1938, was in squadron service by 1940 and continued in production until 1943, by which time 380 aircraft had been flown out of Brough. From 1941 it gave good service for gunnery, navigation and radio training operators based at Silloth and Millom in Cumbria. My father was a communications expert involved in the training of aircrew – many of them Polish – in the use of coded radio and Morse signals. Dad loved the appearance of the Botha and always said that it looked like a modern aeroplane. What the Botha proved to me was the speed at which the Blackburn designs had changed from biplane to monoplane and in the process made so many impressive innovations.

Finally came the Firebrand, the last in the line of the Blackburn aircraft designed and produced during the war, as Eric Mulligan who now lives near Calgary in Canada remembers very well: 'This aircraft allowed me to cut my teeth as a fully fledged airframe and instrument mechanic and I spent time at the Olympia works in Leeds, but especially at Brough. I was fascinated by the Firebrand, formerly known as the Blackburn B-37 but christened from the time it was released from the drawing board. I have read everything about it since its innovations were removed from the secret list. They really did shroud it in great secrecy and we worked surrounded by dire warnings not to discuss the machine outside the assembly line.

'I know that in the main context of your book we are only looking at the secret stuff relating to the war, but don't forget to mention that all these types led up to the jet-propelled Buccaneer which was planned in 1952, flew in 1958 and from 1965 was a mainline weapon for the RAF. It was designed not just for

A Rolls-Royce Merlin engine containing high-quality Sheffield steel.

eye-to-eye combat but also to fire long-range ballistic missiles. The Germans were initially the experts in the field of ballistics but a lot of secret work went on in Yorkshire and elsewhere to combat these missiles, both with regard to their airframes and especially with regard to fuels and ordnance. The Buccaneer would never have been developed had it not been for the Firebrand.'

The Firebrand came into being as a result of an Advisory Design Conference held in 1940 which was chaired by G.E. Petty who was Blackburn's chief designer. The meeting was held in a converted golf clubhouse close to the Brough factory. Petty realised that they had a potential winner with the Firebrand and from this first meeting on 25th July 1940, a prototype was in the air by February 1942. It literally bristled with innovations, including hydraulic flaps, a revolutionary torpedo release mechanism, a new stabilising tail assembly and a compact airscrew which helped to improve the streamlining of the fuselage. The value placed upon this aircraft is indicated by the provision of a new 2,305 horsepower Napier Sabre liquid-cooled engine. This had no fewer than 24 cylinders. Although never so famous as the Rolls-Royce Merlin engine, the Bristol Piston engines reached peaks of power only eventually superseded by the jet engines.

It is quite right that Lancashire should assume a major role in the defeat of the Germans in the air. It is not quite accurate, however, to claim that the development of the jet engine was carried out by Rolls-Royce in Lancashire. The fact is that until the boundary changes of 1974 Barnoldswick, where the huge jet engines are still made, was in Yorkshire. I should apologise yet again for including the Rolls-Royce factory in my two books *Lancashire – the Secret War* and *Memories of the Lancashire Aircraft Industry*, both published by Countryside Books!

In the years before and actually well into the war the future of aero-engines was thought to involve ever more powerful pistons, and jets were considered as nothing but a very minor side show. After all, Rolls-Royce at Derby was producing the ground-breaking Merlin engine which powered both the Spitfire and the Lancaster bomber. There was a demand for more and more Merlins and this led Lord Beaverbrook to set up shadow factories in Barnoldswick and elsewhere and thus ensure that one bombing raid would not cripple the whole production line.

Arthur Redsell at work in the early 1940s.

135

During the course of making BBC radio documentaries I came to know Arthur Redsell, who, in 1996, was living in retirement in Barrowford, which is within a short drive of the Barnoldswick factory. Arthur told me: 'Barnoldswick later took on a life of its own and this is why modern jet engines do not have just 'RR' on their cowlings but 'RRB' which indicates Rolls-Royce Barnoldswick. I first became an apprentice at Derby in 1930 and the only jet I knew was the shiny black stuff you can still buy at Whitby. Piston engines were regarded as the past, present and future of the aircraft industry. None of the workers at Rolls-Royce Derby knew of the battle that Frank Whittle, a serving junior RAF officer, was having with the Air Ministry to get his concept of jet propulsion accepted. He had been given some funding but had spent a lot of his own resources before the Rover Car Company was asked to look into the idea.'

Frank Whittle, never shy to air his opinions, was not happy about Rover in that it was a company which only built car engines and did not have a clue with regard to aero-engines. It took time but eventually the Air Ministry listened and a secret meeting was held at the Swan and Royal Hotel in Clitheroe. Stanley Hooker of Rolls-Royce met the bosses at Rover and it was agreed over dinner in February 1943 that Rolls-Royce would take up the jet engine project in exchange for a tank factory.

Arthur Redsell takes up the story: 'The idea of jet propulsion was still not high on the agenda and this is why young chaps like me were sent to work on the project in what we considered to be the back of beyond somewhere in darkest Yorkshire. The surprise came when we discovered that the jet project was smothered in secrecy and we were shut away in a little place called Bracewell, with its wonderful old church and historic hall. Each day and often through the night we toiled away in an old cotton mill on the outskirts of nearby Clitheroe. We were not part of the main Barnoldswick factory which was hard at work making the Rolls-Royce Merlins, but we soon realised that with luck we would be part of aviation history.'

It was known that the Germans were also working on the

'Men of Jet' – Fred Morley (second right) and Arthur Redsell (first left).

principles of jet propulsion but their focus was radically different. Their scientists used these principles to develop ballistic missiles such as the V1 and V2s. No doubt had the war not ended there would have been even more devastating weapons.

In 1998 I was also able to locate Fred Morley, who was the development engineer for the first Whittle engines and also based at Bracewell. Fred told me in his tough, uncompromising way that, 'Frank Whittle could be an awkward bugger but he knew how to fly aeroplanes and he knew about engines. He gave me a rough time when things did not work out properly but he behaved like a lamb compared to the way he spoke to pinstriped accountants who did not understand why we needed more money. People like me and Arthur [Redsell] worked until we dropped. At first our engine looked like a pile of milk crates and pots and pans all tied up with coloured wire. When you set it going, it sounded like all hell let loose. We told people in the area that we were restoring old tank engines and this was easily accepted. What was not accepted by everybody was the noise we often made during the night. We could not tell 'em that Frank Whittle was coming to see us on the following morning.'

History reveals just how groundbreaking the then new concept of the jet engine was to be. During the war Barnoldswick turned out hundreds of Merlin engines for the Lancaster bomber and Yorkshire also played a major part in building the aircraft itself.

Those passengers using the Leeds Bradford Airport are probably not aware that during the war Yeadon, as it was then called, was a huge aircraft factory. Shrouded as far as it was possible in great secrecy, even the roofs of the buildings were reinforced and turfed over. Cattle and sheep grazed on the roof. From the air the Avro-Yeadon complex would have looked just like another of the many fields which still surround the area. This type of camouflage

was typical of attempts to conceal the factories from the enemy. An RAF squadron, No 609, had been based at Yeadon from 1936 and during the war AVRO produced 4,700 Ansons and 700 Lancasters from this base.

Most of the workforce consisted of women who became very skilful and proud aero-engine fitters. Elsie Stone was one such artisan and she recalls: 'I was an inspector and had to make sure that there was nothing wrong with the engines. We had our own canteen and the food was good. We were not allowed to mix with the other workers because of security. My sister worked in the same factory but I wasn't allowed to see her or talk to her at work. We travelled together on the bus and that was the only time we had

Elsie Stone who worked at Avro Yeadon.

together. We started work at 7 am and finished at 6.30 pm. I started this work when I was 20 and it was my first real job.'

Marie Garside worked shifts with one month on days and the next on nights. She was an electrical inspector working on Lancasters. She recalls that, 'The workers were mostly women which was quite a novelty for the men who worked there. We never saw daylight whilst we were there as it was an underground factory.'

Muriel Kilvington Kay also worked on Lancasters: 'My job was to inspect the electrical wiring on the bomb doors, in the front cabin and on the landing wheels.'

This must have been quite a change for Muriel, who was conscripted and moved from her job in Terry's Chocolate Factory in York to Avro-Yeadon. Women as usual just got on with life and coped. Some girls from Broom Mills in Leeds who trained to weave uniform cloth for the Air Force and Army were uprooted and soon retrained to work in the machine shop at Yeadon. The girls changed from loomers to lathers, whilst Helen Copley, now living in Bramley, began on machines and then become an inspector on the axles of Lancaster bombers.

Most of those who slaved away in the Aero industry found time to relax or they would have gone mad. George Pilkington remembers one incident at Yeadon where work and pleasure mixed, if only for a few minutes: 'I have an everlasting memory as a 16-year-old of working on the bomb bay of a Lancaster and going into work carrying my cricket bag prior to a practice

Sir Roy Dobson. Fancy that! A Yorkshireman designing a Lancaster!

An aerial view of Avro Yeadon, now Leeds Bradford airport.

at the end of my shift. I bumped into a crowd of official-looking chaps including a tubby fella in a posh suit. He walked up to me and talked to me for five minutes about cricket. When he had gone people asked me how I knew Roy Dobson and would I soon get promoted.

'It turned out that he was the boss man who, with Chadwick, had developed the Lancaster. He was a Yorkshire man with the right accent and a love of cricket. I became an AVRO man for life and a bit of an anorak for facts about Yeadon. I found out later that in terms of area it was the company's largest factory, but not

in terms of workers. This record was held by Chadderton but we had 10,240 people, with 7,167 on the day shift and 3,073 hard at it at night. After the war it closed and had industrial units based there but it is now part of the Leeds Bradford Airport complex. I fly out on holiday from what I still call Yeadon and because of the line of the approach the landing is often bumpy. This is not as bumpy, though, as those brave lads flying our Lancs over Germany had to endure. I still treasure my brief chat with the man who later became Sir Roy Dobson.'

It is this irresistible mix of work, play and humour which set Britain apart from all the other European combatants.

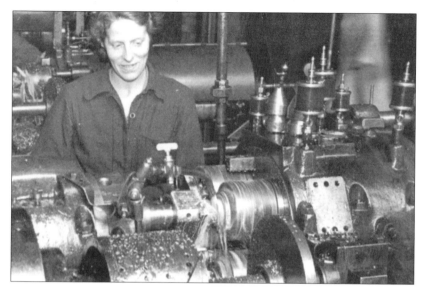

Marie Garside who worked on Lancasters at Yeadon.

Muriel Kilvington Kay at work at Yeadon.

Chapter 8

Work Hard, Play Hard

At the start of the war some, but, thankfully not all elected MPs and career Civil Servants failed to understand that all work and no play made Jack and Jill very dull boys and girls. The decision to close places of entertainment was very soon overturned and the Rugby Football League Committee Minutes of August 1940 recorded the fact that: 'The Ministry of Labour wishes it to be conveyed to the meeting that it desires as much football as possible to be played, so as to provide recreation and relaxation to the workers.'

At this time many active young men were being called up to the services and the two codes of rugby played in the North of England faced the same problem – lack of players, due also to restrictions on movement. Players were allowed to turn out for their nearest club side and the boundaries between the professional Rugby League and the then very strictly amateur Rugby Union were totally blurred (the same rule applied to cricket where the registration of players was relaxed and clubs could allow guests to turn out). In early 1940 the game between Batley and Hull was abandoned after

65 minutes as the sirens sounded and the crowd was diverted into shelters. The space there was so limited and vulnerable that people might have been safer staying where they were.

In early September 1939 the New Zealand Rugby League tourists arrived but after two matches it was obvious that the team would have to be transported home and the tour abandoned. But how? In great secrecy the tourists were gathered together in Harrogate whilst a ship was found for them. In the meantime, the team, made up of tough young men, wanted to do something and they set to work with a will filling sandbags. By mid-September they were aboard the Merchant ship *Rangitika* and avoided the attentions of U-boats to arrive home about six weeks later. Once back in New Zealand many of the team volunteered for the forces and were soon to do battle with the Germans in a much more lethal 'sport'.

Rugby League at war and peace – Eddie Waring.

One man above all others who kept the Rugby League flag flying throughout the war was the Dewsbury journalist Eddie Waring, who managed his home town club throughout the war. At the conclusion of the war Eddie became a household name as a TV commentator on the game and then as one of the hosts in the popular programme *It's a Knockout*. I once heard him say, 'Keeping the game going in the North of England was easy because many young chaps playing were miners and all you had to do to get hold of a pack of tough lads was to shout down the nearest mine shaft.'

The Rugby League tourists setting off for their Australian Tour aboard the aircraft carrier, Indomitable, *in 1946.*

In 1946 the Rugby League authorities sent a touring team to Australia and New Zealand and many players from Yorkshire were transported in safety aboard the aircraft carrier *Indomitable* – this was in a blaze of publicity and without the need for a cloak of secrecy.

Eric Bowes remembers one incident related to sport: 'I was 19 and just come back from being picked up on the Dunkirk beaches. I had a few days' leave and was watching a cricket match at Scarborough. I was sitting next to a reet old fella and I said that I envied those who had nowt to do but play cricket. "Aye, lad," he replied, "I were in the last war but being able to play English cricket is what we both fought for." I have never forgotten that and it sustained me all through the war. As I heard shells exploding in North Africa I kept thinking about cricket and it kept me sane.'

War Work

As hostilities warmed up it really was all hands to the pump and it cannot be emphasised enough how hard women worked and how all the space within the woollen mills was used.

Edith Pearce told me: 'I worked all of my life at Montague Burton on Hudson Road in Leeds. We made uniforms during the war and women were employed as 'feller hands'. This seems a funny job title for a lass but it was the name for a hand sewer. This was tough on the hands but everybody was under pressure to meet targets. Burton's provided us with a restaurant and this eased the pressure on the rations a bit.'

Not every woollen mill wove wool in the war, as Allison Jones told me from her home in Leeds: 'At Fairbairn Lawson Combe Barbour Ltd they changed from making textile machinery to producing massive gun barrels. Women did the work of men and when we finished a shift we had to do our share of fire duty. There

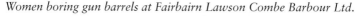

Women boring gun barrels at Fairbairn Lawson Combe Barbour Ltd.

were notices everywhere asking women to do factory work. One strange thing was that some attention was paid to enable us to keep our femininity. Each girl in our factory was issued with a black bag containing our gas mask, some soap, a comb and a wodge of toilet paper. There was a ladies' loo on the roof which seems a strange place to site it. The chaps' loo were in the basement.'

Louise Williams remembers her factory work and travelling on a blacked out bus all the way from Shipley: 'I were at McLarens in Hunslet where we made diesel engines for ships, including submarines, which were sent at night by road either to Cammel Lairds in Birkenhead or to Barrow-in-Furness. I had a friend called Barbara Yates whose father owned lorries. Babs was a huge strong lass and she drove a big lorry loaded with engines to be put into subs. Both of us had real problems because we had no restaurant and had to take sandwiches, which was a real worry with rationing. I was the eldest of seven children and the young ones got priority. I did not worry about this but I was always hungry at work. Barbara loved going to Barrow because she got to know a fisherman near Bardsea and she got a good feed before setting off home.'

Ted Williams told me: 'I were six when the war started and we lived in Knaresborough where my father was a teacher but he got called up. I was brought up by my grandma. I remember that we had a privy at the bottom of the garden and one of my jobs was to cut up newspapers into squares, make holes in the corner with an old knitting needle and push string through to hang on the wall. My first memory of the war was that the paper became thinner and the newspapers also had a lot less pages. I was given a *Dandy* or a *Beano* comic every week but this was also reduced in size and the ink ran because the paper was much thinner.'

It was not only the muscle power of ladies which was needed in the war. The amount of paperwork and red tape which had to be dealt with would have been overwhelming had it not been for a formidable army of women clerks.

Merle Park remembers her days as a clerk: 'I got a job in Darley House on St Paul's Street in Leeds and this was an Army Pay office.

Darley House in St Paul's Street, Leeds was home to an Army Pay Office.

We were told that our work was secret and I suppose it was. The enemy would have loved to have known how many soldiers were being paid and where their money was being sent. There was a sad side to this when we had to work out what was owing to a man who had been killed in order that his family could be paid until the time of his death, after which the pay book was passed on to the pensions department. The temptation was to look at these often battered pay books, but we were under so much pressure that dwelling upon death was very much frowned upon.'

There was also a staff of ladies employed in every town and country district dealing with the issue and checking of ration books, as we saw earlier. Every order for goods and raw materials had to be invoiced and if a government department was involved the invoices had to be done in triplicate and then be checked and rechecked. Likewise there was a mass of paperwork to be processed as each and every farmer recorded his crops and livestock.

Jim Brocklebank who farmed near Richmond told me: 'To be honest it were a bloody nightmare. All our lives we had worked like hell, leaned on a gate when we wanted a rest, paid no attention to writing except when we went to the bank where they helped us out.

Jim Brocklebank, who farmed near Richmond.

Then came the war when we had to count every bloody egg and had to fill in forms to kill an animal. If we got it wrong, the police were on us like a ton of bricks. For most of us our wives did the paperwork, which were sent off to be processed by a load of young lasses who had never mucked out a pigsty in their lives.'

The nature of the paperwork generated changed as the war went on. There was less and less secret data to be kept from the notice of the British people once victory was assured. The ARP and the police kept civilian casualties very much under wraps until long after the war was over. Then details were published of victims of the Blitz including which hospital or mortuary the person was sent to. Leeds, Hull and Sheffield all took something of a beating, but five people were also killed in Huddersfield, three in Rotherham and twelve in Halifax. Lists were published of those working in support of the police including special constables, nursing auxiliaries, those dealing with evacuees and members of what became known as the

Civil Defence Corps. This was a Crown service under the auspices of the Home Office and involved providing detailed reports on six aspects: the anti-invasion headquarters, wardens, rescue services, ambulances, the pioneers whose job it was to clear up rubble, and the welfare services helping those made homeless. A huge number of women were involved here and the WVS (Women's Voluntary Service) did a sterling job.

Elsie Waterson recalls: 'We could turn our hands to owt that was needed. Many of us worked for a time on railway stations. We took over the tea rooms and provided tea and sandwiches for troops who stopped briefly at the station. They occasionally flooded into the rooms but mostly we pushed tea and sandwiches at them in the carriages. They got used to us being there and had their mess tins ready for the brew as cups were in short supply in the war. At one time they made cups without handles to save raw materials, but we were also helped by local people turning up and giving us their spare crockery. Books were also given to us and we handed them to the troops. I remember that after Dunkirk tired lads were being ferried north for a rest but as D-Day got near fresh troops including Yanks all looked ready for the final scrap.'

Most of this book has concerned itself with people working hard and perhaps too little about letting their hair down. In the days before television the cinema was vital and many people wrote to me telling of the smoke-filled buildings like the Ritz, Odeon, Roxy and a host of other evocatively named emporia. The lights of the projector had to penetrate a haze of smoke and the seats smelled of tobacco. Despite this people watched Charlie Chaplin make fun of Hitler and war films predicted the ultimate victory. The Pathe News was heavily censored.

Music and entertainment were provided by radio and the wind-up gramophones which were ideal for use in the shelters. Artists like Vera Lynn were very popular. Vera was not just the Forces' Sweetheart but also the girlfriend of all civilians engaged in their own variant of the war. From the White Cliffs of Dover the waves of the tides of war were turning and victory was in sight by 1943.

Chapter 9

They Think It's All Over – It Is Now!

It became obvious that the tide of war was turning from 1943 onwards: instead of train loads of weary British soldiers coming north, first Italian prisoners of war and soon afterwards German prisoners in increasing numbers were pouring into purpose-built camps.

Even as early as 1942 a small contingent of army personnel under the command of a sergeant arrived at Malton, between York and Scarborough. Their task was to construct a barbed wire enclosure and within this to erect tents to house a steady flow of prisoners of war captured in North Africa. The site was named Eden Camp and the first inmates were 250 Italians. These prisoners were then put to work constructing a larger camp which eventually consisted of 45 wooden huts. There were Italians in residence between 1942 and 1944 and the Germans were incarcerated there from 1944 to as late as 1948. Whilst at the camp the prisoners worked on local farms and were organised by the War Agricultural Officer. After the war the place was largely ignored until 1983 when a local businessman called Stan Johnson saw the potential of Camp 83 and bought it for £750,000. The camp was then largely as it was when the last of 1,200 Germans left for their Fatherland.

During hostilities all German prisoners were interviewed by astute army officers and graded as 'white', 'grey' or 'black'. The white prisoners presented no threat and all were disillusioned by the Nazis and eager for the war to end. In contrast there were those classified as 'black' who still believed in the Hitler philosophy and were waiting for the next lethal weapon to come on-line, bringing with it victory and their return to the way of life of the 1930s. These men had to be closely confined and were held much more securely than was the case at Eden, where 'white' plus a few 'grey' Germans were kept.

Stan Johnson's vision for Eden Camp has worked to perfection and those who read this book will, I hope, be inspired to visit this unique museum. Between 1990 and 1995 the old huts were converted to tell 'The Story of the People's War 1939-1945'. There are huts dealing with Rationing, Saving It, The Red Cross Observer Corps, Women's Land Army and Timber Corps, Civil Defence, Home Guard, Munitions Factories, Women at War, War at Sea, Bomb Disposal and The Bevin Boys.

Thus far the Bevin Boys have not been mentioned even though they played a major role in Yorkshire's war. Colin Sanderson has vivid memories of this aspect of his life: 'I was looking forward to volunteering to join the Navy when I was selected at random to go to work in the coal mines and what a contrast I found as I was sent to a pit in Barnsley instead of a cruiser off Portsmouth which was what I wanted. I had been to grammar school and spoke a bit posh. The miners soon knocked the rough edges off me but there was a real feeling of comradeship down t'pit. I learned to sup ale, swear like a trooper, get mucky, trap rabbits in my spare time, play rugby league and enjoy rude jokes. All this stood me in good stead after the war when I became a schoolteacher working in a tough area of Hull. I could handle all the tough lads and most of the lasses!'

Women also found great changes and I think they were the better for it and were able to enjoy a more equal status after the war. Colin Sanderson takes up the story: 'My sister who also went to a posh school found the war altered her lifestyle. She joined the Land Army and mixed with working folk and discovered that they were just as bright as we were and a damned sight less snobbish. One thing about the war – it was a wonderful leveller. It is a pity that it took such a stressful period to make people aware of it.'

When people had been under threat, first from invasion and then by bombing, in addition to working hard and being told to keep quiet about it, they were good and ready to let their hair down. Not only had they worked harder than ever before but after work they had done fire watches, served in the Home Guard, looked after children, and struggled to put food on the table in the face of rationing. It is no wonder that first VE Day and then VJ Day released the tensions, knowing that first Germany and then Japan were no longer a threat. Parties sprang up all over Britain and food stores jealously guarded over the years were used up all in a hurry.

Winston Churchill visited Leeds in June 1945 and for once everybody knew about it and a good time was had by all. In that same month the Yorkshire Evening Post organised a welcome home party in Roundhay Park for British prisoners of war and some of the airmen who had flown in the Lancasters built at Yeadon turned up in force. The Olympia factory closed in 1946 but its history should never be forgotten even though the site is now occupied by a supermarket.

Street parties were everywhere, every workplace looked like the Christmas to end all Christmases and the police smiled as people got drunk and danced in the street. VE and VJ days were both celebrated by huge bonfires and potatoes were roasted in the ashes as was the rule on bonfire night. Patriotic songs were sung at almost as high a volume as rude songs about the German leaders.

Gladys Bowes, however, has mixed feelings: 'I was a Hull lass and I was six when I was evacuated to near Grassington. I was

VJ celebrations in Leeds.

taken in by a retired schoolmistress who chose me because we shared the same name. Miss Gladys taught me to read and write and made me keep up with my school work. I was sad when the war was over and I had to leave 'Gladys 1', old Yorkie, who was her dog, the little cottage and return home to a terraced house near Hull docks with bomb damage everywhere. My dad had been in the army and my mum had worked in a shell factory and told me that I was talking too posh. Mum and dad were never happy after the war and divorced in 1951. They had lost touch with each other during the war and had been used to regular money coming in. I

Vera Lynn – her records were played over and over again during the war years and were very much a part of the victory celebrations.

visited Miss Gladys very often until she died in her nineties in 1985. By then I had become a qualified teacher, married another teacher and we still refer to our daughter as Gladys 3!'

This story is typical of many families as the euphoria of peace abated whilst rationing continued and jobs were hard to find. But there were many silver linings on the clouds of peace and among these were the dance halls, the radio, the 'filums' as they were called in Yorkshire, and, of course, football and rugby, even if the supporters were mainly confined to men at that time. Huge crowds attended the football and rugby matches and the excursion trains were full of fans. In those days many fans had heavy rattles which would these days be classified as offensive weapons. In the war the sound of a rattle in the streets would have heralded the Germans' use of poison gas.

In this the 21st century, it has become the custom for people to record their activities on the internet, on sites such as Facebook or on Twitter. How much more difficult it would have been to keep secrets in the war had such communications been available! I suppose this book contains the twitterings of those who still remember the part they played in Yorkshire's Secret War. Perhaps this is the time for those who still remember what they were doing in the war to get twittering. Don't worry if you are computer blind, just get your grandchildren to help – they will know just what to do. They may well join with their friends to get Grandma and Grandad on Facebook recording Yorkshire's secret war.

These memories should not be lost and if this book helps just one tiny bit to preserve them it will have been well worth the writing.

Index

INDEX